THIS IS YOUR **PASSBOOK®** FOR ...

OCCUPATIONAL THERAPIST

NLC®

NATIONAL LEARNING CORPORATION®
passbooks.com

COPYRIGHT NOTICE

Copyright © 2020 by

NLC®

National Learning Corporation

212 Michael Drive, Syosset, NY 11791
(516) 921-8888 • www.passbooks.com
E-mail: info@passbooks.com

PUBLISHED IN THE UNITED STATES OF AMERICA

PASSBOOK® SERIES

THE *PASSBOOK® SERIES* has been created to prepare applicants and candidates for the ultimate academic battlefield – the examination room.

At some time in our lives, each and every one of us may be required to take an examination – for validation, matriculation, admission, qualification, registration, certification, or licensure.

Based on the assumption that every applicant or candidate has met the basic formal educational standards, has taken the required number of courses, and read the necessary texts, the *PASSBOOK® SERIES* furnishes the one special preparation which may assure passing with confidence, instead of failing with insecurity. Examination questions – together with answers – are furnished as the basic vehicle for study so that the mysteries of the examination and its compounding difficulties may be eliminated or diminished by a sure method.

This book is meant to help you pass your examination provided that you qualify and are serious in your objective.

The entire field is reviewed through the huge store of content information which is succinctly presented through a provocative and challenging approach – the question-and-answer method.

A climate of success is established by furnishing the correct answers at the end of each test.

You soon learn to recognize types of questions, forms of questions, and patterns of questioning. You may even begin to anticipate expected outcomes.

You perceive that many questions are repeated or adapted so that you can gain acute insights, which may enable you to score many sure points.

You learn how to confront new questions, or types of questions, and to attack them confidently and work out the correct answers.

You note objectives and emphases, and recognize pitfalls and dangers, so that you may make positive educational adjustments.

Moreover, you are kept fully informed in relation to new concepts, methods, practices, and directions in the field.

You discover that you arre actually taking the examination all the time: you are preparing for the examination by "taking" an examination, not by reading extraneous and/or supererogatory textbooks.

In short, this PASSBOOK®, used directedly, should be an important factor in helping you to pass your test.

OCCUPATIONAL THERAPIST

DUTIES

Plans and carries out a program of therapeutic activities prescribed by a physician to facilitate the rehabilitation and employment of physically disabled patients. Instructs physically handicapped patients in arts, crafts, and occupational skills. Evaluates patients' previous employment, training, aptitudes and handicaps. Participates in periodic staff conferences with physicians, nurses, supervising therapists and other medical personnel. Conducts in-service training programs for occupational therapy students and other personnel affiliated with the program. Maintains complete records of each patient's work and progress and makes oral and written reports to the physician in charge. Does related work as required.

EXAMPLES OF TYPICAL TASKS

Assists in evaluation of patient's performance of the activities of daily living; may administer range and motion tests; instructs the disabled in activities of daily living, such as washing, dressing, eating and handling of such corrective devices as braces and wheel chairs; instructs patients in fine and applied arts and certain pre-vocational activities for the purpose of mental and physical re-education; teaches therapeutic arts and crafts, including design in leather, metal, plastics, textiles and wood; assists in setting up programs for the guidance of families with handicapped or disabled members in the home; may instruct student nurses and other personnel in the theory and practice of occupational therapy; assists the Administrator in the development of job descriptions, resident care policies and a procedure manual for the services; treats residents in accordance with appropriate professional practices; integrates the rehabilitation therapy service with all other resident care services; reviews the resident's progress and responses to treatment and revise the treatment plan as necessary; participates in resident care conferences; conducts initial evaluations when ordered by Physician and recommend treatment plan; participates in the selection of additional overtime personnel, assigns duties and provides supervision; maintains equipment, cares for and requisitions supplies; keeps records and makes reports.

HOW TO TAKE A TEST

I. YOU MUST PASS AN EXAMINATION

A. *WHAT EVERY CANDIDATE SHOULD KNOW*

Examination applicants often ask us for help in preparing for the written test. What can I study in advance? What kinds of questions will be asked? How will the test be given? How will the papers be graded?

As an applicant for a civil service examination, you may be wondering about some of these things. Our purpose here is to suggest effective methods of advance study and to describe civil service examinations.

Your chances for success on this examination can be increased if you know how to prepare. Those "pre-examination jitters" can be reduced if you know what to expect. You can even experience an adventure in good citizenship if you know why civil service exams are given.

B. *WHY ARE CIVIL SERVICE EXAMINATIONS GIVEN?*

Civil service examinations are important to you in two ways. As a citizen, you want public jobs filled by employees who know how to do their work. As a job seeker, you want a fair chance to compete for that job on an equal footing with other candidates. The best-known means of accomplishing this two-fold goal is the competitive examination.

Exams are widely publicized throughout the nation. They may be administered for jobs in federal, state, city, municipal, town or village governments or agencies.

Any citizen may apply, with some limitations, such as the age or residence of applicants. Your experience and education may be reviewed to see whether you meet the requirements for the particular examination. When these requirements exist, they are reasonable and applied consistently to all applicants. Thus, a competitive examination may cause you some uneasiness now, but it is your privilege and safeguard.

C. *HOW ARE CIVIL SERVICE EXAMS DEVELOPED?*

Examinations are carefully written by trained technicians who are specialists in the field known as "psychological measurement," in consultation with recognized authorities in the field of work that the test will cover. These experts recommend the subject matter areas or skills to be tested; only those knowledges or skills important to your success on the job are included. The most reliable books and source materials available are used as references. Together, the experts and technicians judge the difficulty level of the questions.

Test technicians know how to phrase questions so that the problem is clearly stated. Their ethics do not permit "trick" or "catch" questions. Questions may have been tried out on sample groups, or subjected to statistical analysis, to determine their usefulness.

Written tests are often used in combination with performance tests, ratings of training and experience, and oral interviews. All of these measures combine to form the best-known means of finding the right person for the right job.

II. HOW TO PASS THE WRITTEN TEST

A. NATURE OF THE EXAMINATION

To prepare intelligently for civil service examinations, you should know how they differ from school examinations you have taken. In school you were assigned certain definite pages to read or subjects to cover. The examination questions were quite detailed and usually emphasized memory. Civil service exams, on the other hand, try to discover your present ability to perform the duties of a position, plus your potentiality to learn these duties. In other words, a civil service exam attempts to predict how successful you will be. Questions cover such a broad area that they cannot be as minute and detailed as school exam questions.

In the public service similar kinds of work, or positions, are grouped together in one "class." This process is known as *position-classification*. All the positions in a class are paid according to the salary range for that class. One class title covers all of these positions, and they are all tested by the same examination.

B. FOUR BASIC STEPS

1) Study the announcement

How, then, can you know what subjects to study? Our best answer is: "Learn as much as possible about the class of positions for which you've applied." The exam will test the knowledge, skills and abilities needed to do the work.

Your most valuable source of information about the position you want is the official exam announcement. This announcement lists the training and experience qualifications. Check these standards and apply only if you come reasonably close to meeting them.

The brief description of the position in the examination announcement offers some clues to the subjects which will be tested. Think about the job itself. Review the duties in your mind. Can you perform them, or are there some in which you are rusty? Fill in the blank spots in your preparation.

Many jurisdictions preview the written test in the exam announcement by including a section called "Knowledge and Abilities Required," "Scope of the Examination," or some similar heading. Here you will find out specifically what fields will be tested.

2) Review your own background

Once you learn in general what the position is all about, and what you need to know to do the work, ask yourself which subjects you already know fairly well and which need improvement. You may wonder whether to concentrate on improving your strong areas or on building some background in your fields of weakness. When the announcement has specified "some knowledge" or "considerable knowledge," or has used adjectives like "beginning principles of..." or "advanced ... methods," you can get a clue as to the number and difficulty of questions to be asked in any given field. More questions, and hence broader coverage, would be included for those subjects which are more important in the work. Now weigh your strengths and weaknesses against the job requirements and prepare accordingly.

3) Determine the level of the position

Another way to tell how intensively you should prepare is to understand the level of the job for which you are applying. Is it the entering level? In other words, is this the position in which beginners in a field of work are hired? Or is it an intermediate or advanced level? Sometimes this is indicated by such words as "Junior" or "Senior" in the class title. Other jurisdictions use Roman numerals to designate the level – Clerk I, Clerk II, for example. The word "Supervisor" sometimes appears in the title. If the level is not indicated by the title, check the description of duties. Will you be working under very close supervision, or will you have responsibility for independent decisions in this work?

4) Choose appropriate study materials

Now that you know the subjects to be examined and the relative amount of each subject to be covered, you can choose suitable study materials. For beginning level jobs, or even advanced ones, if you have a pronounced weakness in some aspect of your training, read a modern, standard textbook in that field. Be sure it is up to date and has general coverage. Such books are normally available at your library, and the librarian will be glad to help you locate one. For entry-level positions, questions of appropriate difficulty are chosen – neither highly advanced questions, nor those too simple. Such questions require careful thought but not advanced training.

If the position for which you are applying is technical or advanced, you will read more advanced, specialized material. If you are already familiar with the basic principles of your field, elementary textbooks would waste your time. Concentrate on advanced textbooks and technical periodicals. Think through the concepts and review difficult problems in your field.

These are all general sources. You can get more ideas on your own initiative, following these leads. For example, training manuals and publications of the government agency which employs workers in your field can be useful, particularly for technical and professional positions. A letter or visit to the government department involved may result in more specific study suggestions, and certainly will provide you with a more definite idea of the exact nature of the position you are seeking.

III. KINDS OF TESTS

Tests are used for purposes other than measuring knowledge and ability to perform specified duties. For some positions, it is equally important to test ability to make adjustments to new situations or to profit from training. In others, basic mental abilities not dependent on information are essential. Questions which test these things may not appear as pertinent to the duties of the position as those which test for knowledge and information. Yet they are often highly important parts of a fair examination. For very general questions, it is almost impossible to help you direct your study efforts. What we can do is to point out some of the more common of these general abilities needed in public service positions and describe some typical questions.

1) General information

Broad, general information has been found useful for predicting job success in some kinds of work. This is tested in a variety of ways, from vocabulary lists to questions about current events. Basic background in some field of work, such as sociology or economics, may be sampled in a group of questions. Often these are principles which have become familiar to most persons through exposure rather than through formal training. It is difficult to advise you how to study for these questions; being alert to the world around you is our best suggestion.

2) Verbal ability

An example of an ability needed in many positions is verbal or language ability. Verbal ability is, in brief, the ability to use and understand words. Vocabulary and grammar tests are typical measures of this ability. Reading comprehension or paragraph interpretation questions are common in many kinds of civil service tests. You are given a paragraph of written material and asked to find its central meaning.

3) Numerical ability

Number skills can be tested by the familiar arithmetic problem, by checking paired lists of numbers to see which are alike and which are different, or by interpreting charts and graphs. In the latter test, a graph may be printed in the test booklet which you are asked to use as the basis for answering questions.

4) Observation

A popular test for law-enforcement positions is the observation test. A picture is shown to you for several minutes, then taken away. Questions about the picture test your ability to observe both details and larger elements.

5) Following directions

In many positions in the public service, the employee must be able to carry out written instructions dependably and accurately. You may be given a chart with several columns, each column listing a variety of information. The questions require you to carry out directions involving the information given in the chart.

6) Skills and aptitudes

Performance tests effectively measure some manual skills and aptitudes. When the skill is one in which you are trained, such as typing or shorthand, you can practice. These tests are often very much like those given in business school or high school courses. For many of the other skills and aptitudes, however, no short-time preparation can be made. Skills and abilities natural to you or that you have developed throughout your lifetime are being tested.

Many of the general questions just described provide all the data needed to answer the questions and ask you to use your reasoning ability to find the answers. Your best preparation for these tests, as well as for tests of facts and ideas, is to be at your physical and mental best. You, no doubt, have your own methods of getting into an exam-taking mood and keeping "in shape." The next section lists some ideas on this subject.

IV. KINDS OF QUESTIONS

Only rarely is the "essay" question, which you answer in narrative form, used in civil service tests. Civil service tests are usually of the short-answer type. Full instructions for answering these questions will be given to you at the examination. But in case this is your first experience with short-answer questions and separate answer sheets, here is what you need to know:

1) Multiple-choice Questions

Most popular of the short-answer questions is the "multiple choice" or "best answer" question. It can be used, for example, to test for factual knowledge, ability to solve problems or judgment in meeting situations found at work.

A multiple-choice question is normally one of three types—

- It can begin with an incomplete statement followed by several possible endings. You are to find the one ending which *best* completes the statement, although some of the others may not be entirely wrong.
- It can also be a complete statement in the form of a question which is answered by choosing one of the statements listed.
- It can be in the form of a problem – again you select the best answer.

Here is an example of a multiple-choice question with a discussion which should give you some clues as to the method for choosing the right answer:

When an employee has a complaint about his assignment, the action which will *best* help him overcome his difficulty is to
- A. discuss his difficulty with his coworkers
- B. take the problem to the head of the organization
- C. take the problem to the person who gave him the assignment
- D. say nothing to anyone about his complaint

In answering this question, you should study each of the choices to find which is best. Consider choice "A" – Certainly an employee may discuss his complaint with fellow employees, but no change or improvement can result, and the complaint remains unresolved. Choice "B" is a poor choice since the head of the organization probably does not know what assignment you have been given, and taking your problem to him is known as "going over the head" of the supervisor. The supervisor, or person who made the assignment, is the person who can clarify it or correct any injustice. Choice "C" is, therefore, correct. To say nothing, as in choice "D," is unwise. Supervisors have and interest in knowing the problems employees are facing, and the employee is seeking a solution to his problem.

2) True/False Questions

The "true/false" or "right/wrong" form of question is sometimes used. Here a complete statement is given. Your job is to decide whether the statement is right or wrong.

SAMPLE: A roaming cell-phone call to a nearby city costs less than a non-roaming call to a distant city.

This statement is wrong, or false, since roaming calls are more expensive.
This is not a complete list of all possible question forms, although most of the others are variations of these common types. You will always get complete directions for

answering questions. Be sure you understand *how* to mark your answers – ask questions until you do.

V. RECORDING YOUR ANSWERS

Computer terminals are used more and more today for many different kinds of exams.

For an examination with very few applicants, you may be told to record your answers in the test booklet itself. Separate answer sheets are much more common. If this separate answer sheet is to be scored by machine – and this is often the case – it is highly important that you mark your answers correctly in order to get credit.

An electronic scoring machine is often used in civil service offices because of the speed with which papers can be scored. Machine-scored answer sheets must be marked with a pencil, which will be given to you. This pencil has a high graphite content which responds to the electronic scoring machine. As a matter of fact, stray dots may register as answers, so do not let your pencil rest on the answer sheet while you are pondering the correct answer. Also, if your pencil lead breaks or is otherwise defective, ask for another.

Since the answer sheet will be dropped in a slot in the scoring machine, be careful not to bend the corners or get the paper crumpled.

The answer sheet normally has five vertical columns of numbers, with 30 numbers to a column. These numbers correspond to the question numbers in your test booklet. After each number, going across the page are four or five pairs of dotted lines. These short dotted lines have small letters or numbers above them. The first two pairs may also have a "T" or "F" above the letters. This indicates that the first two pairs only are to be used if the questions are of the true-false type. If the questions are multiple choice, disregard the "T" and "F" and pay attention only to the small letters or numbers.

Answer your questions in the manner of the sample that follows:

32. The largest city in the United States is
A. Washington, D.C.
B. New York City
C. Chicago
D. Detroit
E. San Francisco

1) Choose the answer you think is best. (New York City is the largest, so "B" is correct.)
2) Find the row of dotted lines numbered the same as the question you are answering. (Find row number 32)
3) Find the pair of dotted lines corresponding to the answer. (Find the pair of lines under the mark "B.")
4) Make a solid black mark between the dotted lines.

VI. BEFORE THE TEST

Common sense will help you find procedures to follow to get ready for an examination. Too many of us, however, overlook these sensible measures. Indeed, nervousness and fatigue have been found to be the most serious reasons why applicants fail to do their best on civil service tests. Here is a list of reminders:

- Begin your preparation early – Don't wait until the last minute to go scurrying around for books and materials or to find out what the position is all about.
- Prepare continuously – An hour a night for a week is better than an all-night cram session. This has been definitely established. What is more, a night a week for a month will return better dividends than crowding your study into a shorter period of time.
- Locate the place of the exam – You have been sent a notice telling you when and where to report for the examination. If the location is in a different town or otherwise unfamiliar to you, it would be well to inquire the best route and learn something about the building.
- Relax the night before the test – Allow your mind to rest. Do not study at all that night. Plan some mild recreation or diversion; then go to bed early and get a good night's sleep.
- Get up early enough to make a leisurely trip to the place for the test – This way unforeseen events, traffic snarls, unfamiliar buildings, etc. will not upset you.
- Dress comfortably – A written test is not a fashion show. You will be known by number and not by name, so wear something comfortable.
- Leave excess paraphernalia at home – Shopping bags and odd bundles will get in your way. You need bring only the items mentioned in the official notice you received; usually everything you need is provided. Do not bring reference books to the exam. They will only confuse those last minutes and be taken away from you when in the test room.
- Arrive somewhat ahead of time – If because of transportation schedules you must get there very early, bring a newspaper or magazine to take your mind off yourself while waiting.
- Locate the examination room – When you have found the proper room, you will be directed to the seat or part of the room where you will sit. Sometimes you are given a sheet of instructions to read while you are waiting. Do not fill out any forms until you are told to do so; just read them and be prepared.
- Relax and prepare to listen to the instructions
- If you have any physical problem that may keep you from doing your best, be sure to tell the test administrator. If you are sick or in poor health, you really cannot do your best on the exam. You can come back and take the test some other time.

VII. AT THE TEST

The day of the test is here and you have the test booklet in your hand. The temptation to get going is very strong. Caution! There is more to success than knowing the right answers. You must know how to identify your papers and understand variations in the type of short-answer question used in this particular examination. Follow these suggestions for maximum results from your efforts:

1) Cooperate with the monitor

The test administrator has a duty to create a situation in which you can be as much at ease as possible. He will give instructions, tell you when to begin, check to see that you are marking your answer sheet correctly, and so on. He is not there to guard you, although he will see that your competitors do not take unfair advantage. He wants to help you do your best.

2) Listen to all instructions

Don't jump the gun! Wait until you understand all directions. In most civil service tests you get more time than you need to answer the questions. So don't be in a hurry. Read each word of instructions until you clearly understand the meaning. Study the examples, listen to all announcements and follow directions. Ask questions if you do not understand what to do.

3) Identify your papers

Civil service exams are usually identified by number only. You will be assigned a number; you must not put your name on your test papers. Be sure to copy your number correctly. Since more than one exam may be given, copy your exact examination title.

4) Plan your time

Unless you are told that a test is a "speed" or "rate of work" test, speed itself is usually not important. Time enough to answer all the questions will be provided, but this does not mean that you have all day. An overall time limit has been set. Divide the total time (in minutes) by the number of questions to determine the approximate time you have for each question.

5) Do not linger over difficult questions

If you come across a difficult question, mark it with a paper clip (useful to have along) and come back to it when you have been through the booklet. One caution if you do this – be sure to skip a number on your answer sheet as well. Check often to be sure that you have not lost your place and that you are marking in the row numbered the same as the question you are answering.

6) Read the questions

Be sure you know what the question asks! Many capable people are unsuccessful because they failed to *read* the questions correctly.

7) Answer all questions

Unless you have been instructed that a penalty will be deducted for incorrect answers, it is better to guess than to omit a question.

8) Speed tests

It is often better NOT to guess on speed tests. It has been found that on timed tests people are tempted to spend the last few seconds before time is called in marking answers at random – without even reading them – in the hope of picking up a few extra points. To discourage this practice, the instructions may warn you that your score will be "corrected" for guessing. That is, a penalty will be applied. The incorrect answers will be deducted from the correct ones, or some other penalty formula will be used.

9) Review your answers

If you finish before time is called, go back to the questions you guessed or omitted to give them further thought. Review other answers if you have time.

10) Return your test materials

If you are ready to leave before others have finished or time is called, take ALL your materials to the monitor and leave quietly. Never take any test material with you. The monitor can discover whose papers are not complete, and taking a test booklet may be grounds for disqualification.

VIII. EXAMINATION TECHNIQUES

1) Read the general instructions carefully. These are usually printed on the first page of the exam booklet. As a rule, these instructions refer to the timing of the examination; the fact that you should not start work until the signal and must stop work at a signal, etc. If there are any *special* instructions, such as a choice of questions to be answered, make sure that you note this instruction carefully.

2) When you are ready to start work on the examination, that is as soon as the signal has been given, read the instructions to each question booklet, underline any key words or phrases, such as *least*, *best*, *outline*, *describe* and the like. In this way you will tend to answer as requested rather than discover on reviewing your paper that you *listed without describing*, that you selected the *worst* choice rather than the *best* choice, etc.

3) If the examination is of the objective or multiple-choice type – that is, each question will also give a series of possible answers: A, B, C or D, and you are called upon to select the best answer and write the letter next to that answer on your answer paper – it is advisable to start answering each question in turn. There may be anywhere from 50 to 100 such questions in the three or four hours allotted and you can see how much time would be taken if you read through all the questions before beginning to answer any. Furthermore, if you come across a question or group of questions which you know would be difficult to answer, it would undoubtedly affect your handling of all the other questions.

4) If the examination is of the essay type and contains but a few questions, it is a moot point as to whether you should read all the questions before starting to answer any one. Of course, if you are given a choice – say five out of seven and the like – then it is essential to read all the questions so you can eliminate the two that are most difficult. If, however, you are asked to answer all the questions, there may be danger in trying to answer the easiest one first because you may find that you will spend too much time on it. The best technique is to answer the first question, then proceed to the second, etc.

5) Time your answers. Before the exam begins, write down the time it started, then add the time allowed for the examination and write down the time it must be completed, then divide the time available somewhat as follows:

- If 3-1/2 hours are allowed, that would be 210 minutes. If you have 80 objective-type questions, that would be an average of 2-1/2 minutes per question. Allow yourself no more than 2 minutes per question, or a total of 160 minutes, which will permit about 50 minutes to review.
- If for the time allotment of 210 minutes there are 7 essay questions to answer, that would average about 30 minutes a question. Give yourself only 25 minutes per question so that you have about 35 minutes to review.

6) The most important instruction is to *read each question* and make sure you know what is wanted. The second most important instruction is to *time yourself properly* so that you answer every question. The third most important instruction is to *answer every question*. Guess if you have to but include something for each question. Remember that you will receive no credit for a blank and will probably receive some credit if you write something in answer to an essay question. If you guess a letter – say "B" for a multiple-choice question – you may have guessed right. If you leave a blank as an answer to a multiple-choice question, the examiners may respect your feelings but it will not add a point to your score. Some exams may penalize you for wrong answers, so in such cases *only*, you may not want to guess unless you have some basis for your answer.

7) Suggestions
    a. Objective-type questions
        1. Examine the question booklet for proper sequence of pages and questions
        2. Read all instructions carefully
        3. Skip any question which seems too difficult; return to it after all other questions have been answered
        4. Apportion your time properly; do not spend too much time on any single question or group of questions
        5. Note and underline key words – *all, most, fewest, least, best, worst, same, opposite,* etc.
        6. Pay particular attention to negatives
        7. Note unusual option, e.g., unduly long, short, complex, different or similar in content to the body of the question
        8. Observe the use of "hedging" words – *probably, may, most likely,* etc.
        9. Make sure that your answer is put next to the same number as the question
        10. Do not second-guess unless you have good reason to believe the second answer is definitely more correct
        11. Cross out original answer if you decide another answer is more accurate; do not erase until you are ready to hand your paper in
        12. Answer all questions; guess unless instructed otherwise
        13. Leave time for review

    b. Essay questions
        1. Read each question carefully
        2. Determine exactly what is wanted. Underline key words or phrases.
        3. Decide on outline or paragraph answer

4. Include many different points and elements unless asked to develop any one or two points or elements
5. Show impartiality by giving pros and cons unless directed to select one side only
6. Make and write down any assumptions you find necessary to answer the questions
7. Watch your English, grammar, punctuation and choice of words
8. Time your answers; don't crowd material

8) Answering the essay question

Most essay questions can be answered by framing the specific response around several key words or ideas. Here are a few such key words or ideas:

M's: manpower, materials, methods, money, management
P's: purpose, program, policy, plan, procedure, practice, problems, pitfalls, personnel, public relations

    a. Six basic steps in handling problems:
      1. Preliminary plan and background development
      2. Collect information, data and facts
      3. Analyze and interpret information, data and facts
      4. Analyze and develop solutions as well as make recommendations
      5. Prepare report and sell recommendations
      6. Install recommendations and follow up effectiveness

    b. Pitfalls to avoid
      1. *Taking things for granted* – A statement of the situation does not necessarily imply that each of the elements is necessarily true; for example, a complaint may be invalid and biased so that all that can be taken for granted is that a complaint has been registered
      2. *Considering only one side of a situation* – Wherever possible, indicate several alternatives and then point out the reasons you selected the best one
      3. *Failing to indicate follow up* – Whenever your answer indicates action on your part, make certain that you will take proper follow-up action to see how successful your recommendations, procedures or actions turn out to be
      4. *Taking too long in answering any single question* – Remember to time your answers properly

IX. AFTER THE TEST

Scoring procedures differ in detail among civil service jurisdictions although the general principles are the same. Whether the papers are hand-scored or graded by machine we have described, they are nearly always graded by number. That is, the person who marks the paper knows only the number – never the name – of the applicant. Not until all the papers have been graded will they be matched with names. If other tests, such as training and experience or oral interview ratings have been given, scores will be combined. Different parts of the examination usually have different weights. For example, the written test might count 60 percent of the final grade, and a rating of training and experience 40 percent. In many jurisdictions, veterans will have a certain number of points added to their grades.

After the final grade has been determined, the names are placed in grade order and an eligible list is established. There are various methods for resolving ties between those who get the same final grade – probably the most common is to place first the name of the person whose application was received first. Job offers are made from the eligible list in the order the names appear on it. You will be notified of your grade and your rank as soon as all these computations have been made. This will be done as rapidly as possible.

People who are found to meet the requirements in the announcement are called "eligibles." Their names are put on a list of eligible candidates. An eligible's chances of getting a job depend on how high he stands on this list and how fast agencies are filling jobs from the list.

When a job is to be filled from a list of eligibles, the agency asks for the names of people on the list of eligibles for that job. When the civil service commission receives this request, it sends to the agency the names of the three people highest on this list. Or, if the job to be filled has specialized requirements, the office sends the agency the names of the top three persons who meet these requirements from the general list.

The appointing officer makes a choice from among the three people whose names were sent to him. If the selected person accepts the appointment, the names of the others are put back on the list to be considered for future openings.

That is the rule in hiring from all kinds of eligible lists, whether they are for typist, carpenter, chemist, or something else. For every vacancy, the appointing officer has his choice of any one of the top three eligibles on the list. This explains why the person whose name is on top of the list sometimes does not get an appointment when some of the persons lower on the list do. If the appointing officer chooses the second or third eligible, the No. 1 eligible does not get a job at once, but stays on the list until he is appointed or the list is terminated.

X. HOW TO PASS THE INTERVIEW TEST

The examination for which you applied requires an oral interview test. You have already taken the written test and you are now being called for the interview test – the final part of the formal examination.

You may think that it is not possible to prepare for an interview test and that there are no procedures to follow during an interview. Our purpose is to point out some things you can do in advance that will help you and some good rules to follow and pitfalls to avoid while you are being interviewed.

What is an interview supposed to test?

The written examination is designed to test the technical knowledge and competence of the candidate; the oral is designed to evaluate intangible qualities, not readily measured otherwise, and to establish a list showing the relative fitness of each candidate – as measured against his competitors – for the position sought. Scoring is not on the basis of "right" and "wrong," but on a sliding scale of values ranging from "not passable" to "outstanding." As a matter of fact, it is possible to achieve a relatively low score without a single "incorrect" answer because of evident weakness in the qualities being measured.

Occasionally, an examination may consist entirely of an oral test – either an individual or a group oral. In such cases, information is sought concerning the technical knowledges and abilities of the candidate, since there has been no written examination for this purpose. More commonly, however, an oral test is used to supplement a written examination.

Who conducts interviews?

The composition of oral boards varies among different jurisdictions. In nearly all, a representative of the personnel department serves as chairman. One of the members of the board may be a representative of the department in which the candidate would work. In some cases, "outside experts" are used, and, frequently, a businessman or some other representative of the general public is asked to serve. Labor and management or other special groups may be represented. The aim is to secure the services of experts in the appropriate field.

However the board is composed, it is a good idea (and not at all improper or unethical) to ascertain in advance of the interview who the members are and what groups they represent. When you are introduced to them, you will have some idea of their backgrounds and interests, and at least you will not stutter and stammer over their names.

What should be done before the interview?

While knowledge about the board members is useful and takes some of the surprise element out of the interview, there is other preparation which is more substantive. It *is* possible to prepare for an oral interview – in several ways:

1) Keep a copy of your application and review it carefully before the interview

This may be the only document before the oral board, and the starting point of the interview. Know what education and experience you have listed there, and the sequence and dates of all of it. Sometimes the board will ask you to review the highlights of your experience for them; you should not have to hem and haw doing it.

2) Study the class specification and the examination announcement

Usually, the oral board has one or both of these to guide them. The qualities, characteristics or knowledges required by the position sought are stated in these documents. They offer valuable clues as to the nature of the oral interview. For example, if the job involves supervisory responsibilities, the announcement will usually indicate that knowledge of modern supervisory methods and the qualifications of the candidate as a supervisor will be tested. If so, you can expect such questions, frequently in the form of a hypothetical situation which you are expected to solve. NEVER go into an oral without knowledge of the duties and responsibilities of the job you seek.

3) Think through each qualification required

Try to visualize the kind of questions you would ask if you were a board member. How well could you answer them? Try especially to appraise your own knowledge and background in each area, *measured against the job sought*, and identify any areas in which you are weak. Be critical and realistic – do not flatter yourself.

4) Do some general reading in areas in which you feel you may be weak

For example, if the job involves supervision and your past experience has NOT, some general reading in supervisory methods and practices, particularly in the field of human relations, might be useful. Do NOT study agency procedures or detailed manuals. The oral board will be testing your understanding and capacity, not your memory.

5) Get a good night's sleep and watch your general health and mental attitude

You will want a clear head at the interview. Take care of a cold or any other minor ailment, and of course, no hangovers.

What should be done on the day of the interview?

Now comes the day of the interview itself. Give yourself plenty of time to get there. Plan to arrive somewhat ahead of the scheduled time, particularly if your appointment is in the fore part of the day. If a previous candidate fails to appear, the board might be ready for you a bit early. By early afternoon an oral board is almost invariably behind schedule if there are many candidates, and you may have to wait. Take along a book or magazine to read, or your application to review, but leave any extraneous material in the waiting room when you go in for your interview. In any event, relax and compose yourself.

The matter of dress is important. The board is forming impressions about you – from your experience, your manners, your attitude, and your appearance. Give your personal appearance careful attention. Dress your best, but not your flashiest. Choose conservative, appropriate clothing, and be sure it is immaculate. This is a business interview, and your appearance should indicate that you regard it as such. Besides, being well groomed and properly dressed will help boost your confidence.

Sooner or later, someone will call your name and escort you into the interview room. *This is it.* From here on you are on your own. It is too late for any more preparation. But remember, you asked for this opportunity to prove your fitness, and you are here because your request was granted.

What happens when you go in?

The usual sequence of events will be as follows: The clerk (who is often the board stenographer) will introduce you to the chairman of the oral board, who will introduce you to the other members of the board. Acknowledge the introductions before you sit down. Do not be surprised if you find a microphone facing you or a stenotypist sitting by. Oral interviews are usually recorded in the event of an appeal or other review.

Usually the chairman of the board will open the interview by reviewing the highlights of your education and work experience from your application – primarily for the benefit of the other members of the board, as well as to get the material into the record. Do not interrupt or comment unless there is an error or significant misinterpretation; if that is the case, do not hesitate. But do not quibble about insignificant matters. Also, he will usually ask you some question about your education, experience or your present job – partly to get you to start talking and to establish the interviewing "rapport." He may start the actual questioning, or turn it over to one of the other members. Frequently, each member undertakes the questioning on a particular area, one in which he is perhaps most competent, so you can expect each member to participate in the examination. Because time is limited, you may also expect some rather abrupt switches in the direction the questioning takes, so do not be upset by it. Normally, a board member will not pursue a single line of questioning unless he discovers a particular strength or weakness.

After each member has participated, the chairman will usually ask whether any member has any further questions, then will ask you if you have anything you wish to add. Unless you are expecting this question, it may floor you. Worse, it may start you off on an extended, extemporaneous speech. The board is not usually seeking more information. The question is principally to offer you a last opportunity to present further qualifications or to indicate that you have nothing to add. So, if you feel that a significant qualification or characteristic has been overlooked, it is proper to point it out in a sentence or so. Do not compliment the board on the thoroughness of their examination – they have been sketchy, and you know it. If you wish, merely say, "No thank you, I have nothing further to add." This is a point where you can "talk yourself out" of a good impression or fail to present an important bit of information. Remember, *you close the interview yourself.*

The chairman will then say, "That is all, Mr. _____, thank you." Do not be startled; the interview is over, and quicker than you think. Thank him, gather your belongings and take your leave. Save your sigh of relief for the other side of the door.

How to put your best foot forward

Throughout this entire process, you may feel that the board individually and collectively is trying to pierce your defenses, seek out your hidden weaknesses and embarrass and confuse you. Actually, this is not true. They are obliged to make an appraisal of your qualifications for the job you are seeking, and they want to see you in your best light. Remember, they must interview all candidates and a non-cooperative candidate may become a failure in spite of their best efforts to bring out his qualifications. Here are 15 suggestions that will help you:

1) Be natural – Keep your attitude confident, not cocky

If you are not confident that you can do the job, do not expect the board to be. Do not apologize for your weaknesses, try to bring out your strong points. The board is interested in a positive, not negative, presentation. Cockiness will antagonize any board member and make him wonder if you are covering up a weakness by a false show of strength.

2) Get comfortable, but don't lounge or sprawl

Sit erectly but not stiffly. A careless posture may lead the board to conclude that you are careless in other things, or at least that you are not impressed by the importance of the occasion. Either conclusion is natural, even if incorrect. Do not fuss with your clothing, a pencil or an ashtray. Your hands may occasionally be useful to emphasize a point; do not let them become a point of distraction.

3) Do not wisecrack or make small talk

This is a serious situation, and your attitude should show that you consider it as such. Further, the time of the board is limited – they do not want to waste it, and neither should you.

4) Do not exaggerate your experience or abilities

In the first place, from information in the application or other interviews and sources, the board may know more about you than you think. Secondly, you probably will not get away with it. An experienced board is rather adept at spotting such a situation, so do not take the chance.

5) If you know a board member, do not make a point of it, yet do not hide it

Certainly you are not fooling him, and probably not the other members of the board. Do not try to take advantage of your acquaintanceship – it will probably do you little good.

6) Do not dominate the interview

Let the board do that. They will give you the clues – do not assume that you have to do all the talking. Realize that the board has a number of questions to ask you, and do not try to take up all the interview time by showing off your extensive knowledge of the answer to the first one.

7) Be attentive

You only have 20 minutes or so, and you should keep your attention at its sharpest throughout. When a member is addressing a problem or question to you, give him your undivided attention. Address your reply principally to him, but do not exclude the other board members.

8) Do not interrupt

A board member may be stating a problem for you to analyze. He will ask you a question when the time comes. Let him state the problem, and wait for the question.

9) Make sure you understand the question

Do not try to answer until you are sure what the question is. If it is not clear, restate it in your own words or ask the board member to clarify it for you. However, do not haggle about minor elements.

10) Reply promptly but not hastily

A common entry on oral board rating sheets is "candidate responded readily," or "candidate hesitated in replies." Respond as promptly and quickly as you can, but do not jump to a hasty, ill-considered answer.

11) Do not be peremptory in your answers

A brief answer is proper – but do not fire your answer back. That is a losing game from your point of view. The board member can probably ask questions much faster than you can answer them.

12) Do not try to create the answer you think the board member wants

He is interested in what kind of mind you have and how it works – not in playing games. Furthermore, he can usually spot this practice and will actually grade you down on it.

13) Do not switch sides in your reply merely to agree with a board member

Frequently, a member will take a contrary position merely to draw you out and to see if you are willing and able to defend your point of view. Do not start a debate, yet do not surrender a good position. If a position is worth taking, it is worth defending.

14) Do not be afraid to admit an error in judgment if you are shown to be wrong

The board knows that you are forced to reply without any opportunity for careful consideration. Your answer may be demonstrably wrong. If so, admit it and get on with the interview.

15) Do not dwell at length on your present job

The opening question may relate to your present assignment. Answer the question but do not go into an extended discussion. You are being examined for a *new* job, not your present one. As a matter of fact, try to phrase ALL your answers in terms of the job for which you are being examined.

Basis of Rating

Probably you will forget most of these "do's" and "don'ts" when you walk into the oral interview room. Even remembering them all will not ensure you a passing grade. Perhaps you did not have the qualifications in the first place. But remembering them will help you to put your best foot forward, without treading on the toes of the board members.

Rumor and popular opinion to the contrary notwithstanding, an oral board wants you to make the best appearance possible. They know you are under pressure – but they also want to see how you respond to it as a guide to what your reaction would be under the pressures of the job you seek. They will be influenced by the degree of poise you display, the personal traits you show and the manner in which you respond.

ABOUT THIS BOOK

This book contains tests divided into Examination Sections. Go through each test, answering every question in the margin. At the end of each test look at the answer key and check your answers. On the ones you got wrong, look at the right answer choice and learn. Do not fill in the answers first. Do not memorize the questions and answers, but understand the answer and principles involved. On your test, the questions will likely be different from the samples. Questions are changed and new ones added. If you understand these past questions you should have success with any changes that arise. Tests may consist of several types of questions. We have additional books on each subject should more study be advisable or necessary for you. Finally, the more you study, the better prepared you will be. This book is intended to be the last thing you study before you walk into the examination room. Prior study of relevant texts is also recommended. NLC publishes some of these in our Fundamental Series. Knowledge and good sense are important factors in passing your exam. Good luck also helps. So now study this Passbook, absorb the material contained within and take that knowledge into the examination. Then do your best to pass that exam.

EXAMINATION SECTION

EXAMINATION SECTION
TEST 1

DIRECTIONS: Each question or incomplete statement is followed by several suggested answers or completions. Select the one that BEST answers the question or completes the statement. *PRINT THE LETTER OF THE CORRECT ANSWER IN THE SPACE AT THE RIGHT.*

1. To minimize the distress of a confused, disoriented person, the occupational therapist should

    A. accept the person as is
    B. encourage decision-making
    C. decrease distracting stimuli
    D. provide for creative outlets

    1.____

2. A patient being treated for an injury that severed the median nerve three inches above the wrist will have difficulty with

    A. supination and pronation
    B. wrist extension
    C. finger extension
    D. thumb opposition

    2.____

3. Which of the following BEST facilitates spinal extension and stimulates integration of the tonic labyrinthine reflex?

    A. Crawling through a maze
    B. Walking on a balance beam
    C. Rolling in a carpeted barrel
    D. Riding prone on a scooter board

    3.____

4. What is the MOST important consideration in assessing a patient's employability?

    A. Endurance
    B. Work habits
    C. Coordination
    D. Intelligence

    4.____

5. In assessing cognitive levels according to Piaget, which of the following options represents the HIGHEST development?

    A. Preoperational
    B. Sensorimotor
    C. Abstract formal
    D. Concrete operations

    5.____

6. In a Problem-Oriented Medical Record, a progress note entry that reads: *Patient reaches overhead to a height of six feet and is able to dress independently* is an example of a(n)

    A. assessment
    B. treatment plan
    C. objective finding
    D. subjective finding

    6.____

7. What should be the FIRST step in developing a new occupational therapy service in a home health program?

    A. Planning a budget
    B. Completing a needs assessment
    C. Establishing program goals
    D. Identifying reimbursement sources

    7.____

Questions 8-10.

DIRECTIONS: Questions 8 through 10 are to be answered on the basis of the following information.

A seventeen-year-old male, injured in a gang fight eight weeks ago, sustained a complete transection of the spinal cord at the T5-6 level. The gang members continued to
threaten him following his admission to the rehabilitation facility.

8. Prior to transfer activities, emphasis should be placed on strengthening his   8.____

   A. rhomboids   B. latissimus dorsi
   C. levator scapulae   D. serratus anterior

9. To put on his trousers, the BEST method for this patient to use is to   9.____

   A. roll from side to side in bed
   B. shift from side to side on his wheelchair
   C. sit on a bed with his legs over the side of the bed
   D. sit in his wheelchair with his legs propped on a bed

10. The patient frequently expresses great concern about future attacks from the gang mem-   10.____
    bers and needs constant assurance that the security guard is on duty.
    His concern is based on

   A. reality testing   B. neurotic anxiety
   C. ideas of reference   D. grandiose ideation

11. When instructed to put on his shoes, a patient has no difficulty putting on and fastening   11.____
    his right shoe. He neglects his left foot completely and tells the occupational therapist
    that he has completed the task.
    Which of the following systems should be evaluated to determine the cause of this
    behavior?

   A. Motor   B. Sensory   C. Vestibular   D. Limbic

12. If a patient is asked to give the meaning of a proverb, he is being asked to demonstrate   12.____
    his

   A. memory   B. thought
   C. affective awareness   D. conceptual ability

13. In the supervisory session, it is the responsibility of the supervisee to   13.____

   A. accept the directions of the supervisor
   B. communicate learning needs honestly
   C. prepare an objective report on own performance
   D. list the events of interactions with patients

14. Which of the following facilitation techniques is appropriate to use with a four-year-old   14.____
    with hypotonicity resulting from damage to the central nervous system?

   A. Bouncing on knee
   B. Wrapping in a blanket
   C. Gentle rhythmical rocking
   D. Slow stroking down each side of the vertebral column

KEY (CORRECT ANSWERS)

1.	C		6.	C
2.	D		7.	B
3.	D		8.	B
4.	B		9.	A
5.	C		10.	A

11.	B
12.	D
13.	B
14.	A

———

EXAMINATION SECTION
TEST 1

DIRECTIONS: Each question or incomplete statement is followed by several suggested answers or completions. Select the one that BEST answers the question or completes the statement. *PRINT THE LETTER OF THE CORRECT ANSWER IN THE SPACE AT THE RIGHT.*

1. All of the following patients should have sensory evaluation for occupational therapy EXCEPT those with   1.____

    A. burns   B. fractures
    C. peptic ulcers   D. spinal cord injuries
    E. neurological diseases

2. While evaluating a patient for occupational therapy, the assessment of coordination will check the ability   2.____

    A. of a group of muscles to work together to perform a task
    B. to follow directions
    C. to produce verbal and social skills
    D. to handle the activities given in occupational therapy
    E. none of the above

3. While evaluating for occupational therapy, during endurance testing, a person is tested for   3.____

    A. all activities a person does for enjoyment
    B. ability to reach or maintain the energy output necessary to perform an activity
    C. ability to perform activities of daily life
    D. coordination
    E. none of the above

4. When a patient is observed during the performance of activities of daily life, it is called _____ assessment.   4.____

    A. functional   B. endurance
    C. coordination   D. physical capacities
    E. self-maintenance

5. While evaluating a patient for occupational therapy, the physical capacities evaluation should summarize the patient's _____ in all the activities tested.   5.____

    A. ability   B. endurance
    C. speed   D. safety
    E. all of the above

6. A cognitive component of performance determines whether the patient can   6.____

    A. attend a task in order to learn it
    B. attend a task in order to perform it
    C. solve problems
    D. remember information over short and long periods of time
    E. all of the above

7. All of the following are adaptive techniques used with patients with impairments in passive and active range of motion in the upper extremities EXCEPT

    A. using one upper extremity to assist the other in reaching to the mouth
    B. resting the elbow on a high surface to allow reaching to the mouth
    C. modification of food consistency
    D. using both hands to hold a cup or glass
    E. using tenodesis to pick up a glass

7.____

8. Grooming disabilities can result from the INABILITY to

    A. reach face, all areas of head, and faucets
    B. pick up, hold, and manipulate brush, razor, and other tools
    C. use both hands simultaneously to open a container or file nails
    D. attend to the activity, locate the items needed, and use them appropriately
    E. all of the above

8.____

9. A patient is referred to you with impairments in active and passive range of motion in the upper extremities and neck.
What adaptive techniques would you use with this patient?

    A. Assisting one extremity with the other to improve reach, and using mouth to open containers
    B. Using liquid soap in push-button dispenser
    C. Modifying hairstyle to eliminate need for setting
    D. All of the above
    E. None of the above

9.____

10. A patient is referred to you for evaluation of occupational therapy.
The INITIAL assessment of productivity should include the ability to

    A. follow directions
    B. use judgment
    C. be punctual
    D. exercise certain skills
    E. all of the above

10.____

11. The geriatric patients rating scale is designed to help in planning treatment programs.
The areas rated include
      I. physical capabilities
     II. self-care skills
    III. social interaction skills
The CORRECT answer is:

    A. I only   B. I, II, III   C. II, III
    D. I, III   E. III only

11.____

12. Sensory testing is frequently performed when evaluating patients with physical dysfunctions.
In patients with burns, fractures, and spinal cord injuries, the areas tested include

    A. light touch and moving touch
    B. pain
    C. temperature

12.____

D. vibratory sense
E. all of the above

13. Feeding disabilities in patients can result from the inability to   13.____
     I.   swallow food and drink safely
    II.   reach hand to the mouth
   III.   pick up and hold utensils, finger foods, and beverage containers
   IV.   use both hands simultaneously to cut food
The CORRECT answer is:

A. I, II, III, IV   B. II, IV   C. II, III, IV
D. I, II, III   E. I, III

14. Which of the following adaptive techniques may be used with impairments in range,   14.____
strength, and coordination of oral musculature?

A. Head, neck, and body positioning to facilitate proper swallowing
B. Modification of food consistency
C. Positioning equipment to maintain a suitable position
D. All of the above
E. None of the above

15. All of the following psychological tests are used to test achievement and reading during   15.____
work assessment EXCEPT

A. adult basic learning examination
B. draw a person test
C. Gray oral reading test
D. California achievement test
E. Nelson-Denny reading test

16. The draw-a-person test is specifically used to test   16.____

A. achievement   B. intelligence
C. personality   D. vocational aptitudes
E. reading

17. While doing work assessment, all of the following tests are used to assess vocational   17.____
interests EXCEPT the

A. Strong vocational interest bank
B. Geist picture interest inventory
C. Purdue pegboard
D. Minnesota importance questionnaire
E. wide range interest opinion test

18. The McCarron-Dial System is a work evaluation system.   18.____
This system is targeted for patients with

A. learning disabilities   B. mental retardation
C. social handicaps   D. cerebral palsy
E. all of the above

19. The Azima Battery is a psychological test which assesses   19.____

    A. mood organization   B. organization of drives
    C. ego organization   D. object relations
    E. all of the above

20. The Goodenough-Harris drawing test is used to test   20.____

    A. verbal intelligence
    B. effectiveness in coping with environmental demands
    C. accuracy of observation and development of conceptual thinking
    D. drawing skills
    E. none of the above

21. The Lincoln-Oseretsky motor developmental scale is often used by therapists to evaluate   21.____

    A. dexterity of hand
    B. hand and arm movement
    C. hand and arm movements measuring speed, dexterity, coordination, and rhythm
    D. coordination of hand
    E. none of the above

22. Which of the following tests is OFTEN used to evaluate activities of daily life (ADL)?   22.____

    A. Purdue pegboard
    B. Box and block test
    C. Brigan screen
    D. Jebsen Taylor hand function test
    E. None of the above

23. The Purdue pegboard test is used to aid in the selection of employees for _____ jobs.   23.____

    A. packing   B. industrial
    C. landscaping   D. teaching
    E. none of the above

24. When an employee is injured on the job, the cost of the injury can be great.   24.____
Who NORMALLY pays for all medical and physical rehabilitation expenses incurred in treating the injury?

    A. Employee
    B. Workmen's compensation insurance carrier
    C. Government
    D. Physical therapist
    E. Employees' union

25. A person's job is defined as minimum lifting of papers, small tools or file folders, maximum lift of 10 lbs., requires occasional walking or standing.   25.____
How would you classify this work level?
_____ work.

    A. Sedentary   B. Light   C. Medium
    D. Heavy   E. Very heavy

KEY (CORRECT ANSWERS)

1.	C	11.	B
2.	A	12.	E
3.	B	13.	A
4.	A	14.	D
5.	E	15.	B
6.	E	16.	C
7.	C	17.	C
8.	E	18.	E
9.	D	19.	E
10.	E	20.	C

21.	C
22.	D
23.	B
24.	B
25.	A

TEST 2

DIRECTIONS: Each question or incomplete statement is followed by several suggested answers or completions. Select the one that BEST answers the question or completes the statement. *PRINT THE LETTER OF THE CORRECT ANSWER IN THE SPACE AT THE RIGHT.*

1. All of the following should be included while evaluating the productivity of a patient for occupational therapy EXCEPT

    A. skills in certain work settings
    B. ability to follow directions
    C. ability to judge the situation
    D. performance of certain skills
    E. ability of self-grooming

1.____

2. The _____ component of performance evaluation is normally evaluated to check the basic movement required for occupational therapy.

    A. sensory   B. motor
    C. cognitive   D. interpersonal
    E. none of the above

2.____

3. The _____ component of performance is evaluated to see the patient's ability to distinguish reality from unreality and to deal with reality.

    A. motor   B. cognitive
    C. intrapersonal   D. sensory
    E. intellectual

3.____

4. The _____ component of performance evaluation would tell the therapist the ability of the patient to relate and to get along with other people.

    A. motor   B. behavioral
    C. interpersonal   D. intrapersonal
    E. cognitive

4.____

5. An occupational therapist must meet two essential requirements to conduct a successful interview: solid knowledge base to select questions and areas to be covered, and

    A. tell the parents about your experience
    B. realize the outcome or conclusion of the interview immediately
    C. active listening skills
    D. plan the treatment immediately
    E. tell patient and parent about your qualifications

5.____

6. To maintain reliability and accuracy each time a patient's range of motion is tested, it should be measured _____ every time.

    A. by the same therapist
    B. using the same method
    C. at the same time of the day
    D. all of the above
    E. none of the above

6.____

7. _____ muscle movement is used to evaluate muscle tone.   7.____

    A. Active   B. Passive
    C. Active resistive   D. Passive resistive
    E. None of the above

8. If the muscle tone is decreased, there will be a DECREASED resistance to _____   8.____
movement.

    A. passive   B. active
    C. gravitational   D. free
    E. none of the above

9. A reflex is an involuntary stereotyped response to a particular stimulus that is developed   9.____
in fetal life and continues to dominate motor behavior through

    A. childhood   B. the neonatal period
    C. early infancy   D. early adolescence
    E. early adulthood

10. Which of the following factors is very important while evaluating the reflexes and label-   10.____
ing them as normal or abnormal?

    A. Hyperactivity or hypoactivity of a reflex
    B. Diagnosis
    C. Mental status
    D. Age of the individual
    E. None of the above

11. All of the following are true regarding meningocoele EXCEPT: 11.____

    A. It involves meninges only
    B. It may require neurosurgical excision
    C. It causes no orthopedic problems
    D. It causes neurological abnormalities
    E. Children rarely need occupational therapy

12. Myelomeningocoele is characterized by all of the following EXCEPT: 12.____

    A. Actual etiology is unknown
    B. Defects occur between the third and fourth weeks of gestation
    C. Risk of having a second child with a neural tube defect is about 10 percent
    D. Associated with increased levels of alpha-fetoprotein in amniotic fluid
    E. Presents with multiple neurologic problems

13. A malformation of the posterior fossae, which frequently occurs in children with neural   13.____
tube defect, is known as

    A. hydrocephalus
    B. hydrosyringomyelia
    C. arteriovenous malformation
    D. tethered cord
    E. Arnold-Chiari deformity

14. The MOST common neurologic concern in patients with myelomeningocoele is   14.____

    A. hydrocephalus
    B. hydrosyringomyelia
    C. Arnold-Chiari malformation
    D. tethered cord
    E. neurogenic bladder

15. A physiologic or biochemical restriction in the information processing capacities of the   15.____
brain which produces observable, measurable limitations in routine task behavior is
known as

    A. behavior dysfunction
    B. developmental disability
    C. cognitive disability
    D. mental disability
    E. none of the above

16. Which of the following tests is used by the therapist to measure manual dexterity?   16.____

    A. Jebsen Taylor hand function test
    B. Box and block test
    C. Callier-Azusa scale
    D. Goodman battery
    E. All of the above

17. All of the following tests can be used by a therapist to evaluate motor functions and man-   17.____
ual dexterity EXCEPT the

    A. Purdue pegboard
    B. Jebsen Taylor hand function test
    C. box and block test
    D. Callier-Azusa scale
    E. none of the above

18. The comprehensive occupational therapy evaluation assesses 25 different identified   18.____
behaviors in all of the following areas EXCEPT

    A. general   B. interpersonal
    C. task performance   D. intelligence
    E. none of the above

19. The Bay area functional performance evaluation (BAFPE) assesses functional perfor-   19.____
mance in

    A. activities of daily life in normal individuals
    B. activities of daily life in psychiatric clients
    C. stressful situations
    D. business life
    E. all of the above

20. To determine whether home or family management will be an appropriate focal area of   20._____
treatment, the therapist interviews the patient and the patient's family to obtain information about all of the following areas EXCEPT the patient's

    A.   education
    B.   living circumstances
    C.   family background, goals, and values
    D.   available resources
    E.   none of the above

21. While determining whether home and family management should be a focus of occupa-   21._____
tional therapy intervention, it is IMPORTANT to include the _____ of the patient to find
out about the patient's role of home maintainer or caregiver.

    A.   occupational history
    B.   past, present, and future roles
    C.   daily and weekly schedule
    D.   all of the above
    E.   none of the above

22. All of the following are tools that can be used to gather data related to the role of home   22._____
maintainer or caregiver about a patient who may need home and family management
EXCEPT the

    A.   role checklist
    B.   available resources
    C.   pie of life form
    D.   activity configuration form
    E.   none of the above

23. All of the following are approaches to the assessment of home management and care-   23._____
giver tasks EXCEPT

    A.   direct observation of specific patient performance
    B.   give a questionnaire to a caregiver
    C.   self-administered questionnaire
    D.   evaluation of performance components
    E.   none of the above

24. Which of the following is NOT an advantage of the direct observation approach to assess   24._____
home management tasks?

    A.   Most direct means of assessing functional performance
    B.   Can detect faulty and/or unsafe methods easily
    C.   Presence of examiner may affect the results
    D.   Reliable and valid scores obtained when tests are standardized or protocol defined
    E.   None of the above

25. The Kohlman evaluation of living skills is designed to evaluate 25.____
    A. a normal individual's ability to function safely
    B. mental capabilities of a disabled individual
    C. intelligence of normal individuals
    D. intelligence in psychiatric patients
    E. a psychiatric patient's ability to function safely and independently in the community

---

KEY (CORRECT ANSWERS)

1.	E	11.	D
2.	B	12.	C
3.	C	13.	E
4.	C	14.	A
5.	C	15.	C
6.	D	16.	B
7.	B	17.	D
8.	A	18.	D
9.	C	19.	B
10.	D	20.	A

21.	D
22.	B
23.	B
24.	C
25.	E

EXAMINATION SECTION
TEST 1

DIRECTIONS: Each question or incomplete statement is followed by several suggested answers or completions. Select the one that BEST answers the question or completes the statement. *PRINT THE LETTER OF THE CORRECT ANSWER IN THE SPACE AT THE RIGHT.*

1. The test used to evaluate the neonate's reaction to stimuli and responses to the environment is the

    A. Denver developmental screening test
    B. Brazelton behavioral assessment scale
    C. Callier-Azusa scale
    D. box and block test
    E. Bayley scales

1.____

2. The MOST useful test to evaluate mentally retarded individuals is the

    A. Bender-Gestalt test
    B. adaptive behavior scale
    C. Vineland social maturity scale
    D. Allen cognitive level
    E. none of the above

2.____

3. The Miller TIME test is used for psychological, psychiatric, and cognitive assessment of children.
All of the following are true of the Miller-Time test EXCEPT:

    A. demonstrates developmental delays
    B. risks of motor dysfunction
    C. demonstrates dysfunctional positions
    D. can be tested in a 10 year old
    E. none of the above

3.____

4. The infant/toddler scale for everyday (ITSE) is administered by a partnership of parents and professionals in which the parent elicits play as the examiner observes and scores the child for developmental assessment.
This test is for children from age _____ months.

    A. birth to 3   B. birth to 6
    C. 3 months to 42   D. 3 months to 6
    E. birth to 42

4.____

5. The MOST common *inherited* cause of mental retardation is

    A. Turner syndrome   B. Down's syndrome
    C. Fragile X syndrome   D. Cri du chat syndrome
    E. phenylketonuria

5.____

6. All of the following are causes of mental retardation EXCEPT

    A. genetic
    B. metabolic

6.____

   C.   congenital infections
   D.   trauma
   E.   familial or environmental

7.   While planning treatment for mentally retarded individuals, the philosophy of normalization suggests that persons with mental retardation   7._____

   A.   should study with normal children in regular schools
   B.   are best served when they experience everyday (normal) life
   C.   should be considered normal
   D.   should not be given any help
   E.   may not become normal

8.   The developmental treatment approach for a child with mental retardation   8._____

   A.   simulates learning experiences that result in acquisition during normal development
   B.   is based on sensorimotor treatment
   C.   states that comprehensive knowledge of developmental flow of different components of function is not necessary
   D.   does not use technology
   E.   is similar to the behavioral approach

9.   A patient with cerebral palsy in both upper and lower extremities with mild upper involvement is said to have   9._____

   A.   monoplegia   B.   hemiplegia
   C.   diplegia   D.   paraplegia
   E.   quadriplegia

10.   A 4 year-old child who had E. coli meningitis in the neonatal period is now quadriplegic. This means that   10._____

   A.   one extremity is involved
   B.   two extremities are involved
   C.   the upper and lower extremities on one side are involved
   D.   there is equal involvement of both upper and lower extremities
   E.   both upper and lower extremities are involved, with mild upper involvement

11.   About 25% of all children with cerebral palsy show fluctuating muscle tone and purposeless movements, which are caused by damage to the   11._____

   A.   frontal lobe   B.   parietal lobe
   C.   basal ganglia   D.   midbrain
   E.   occipital lobe

12.   About 50% of children with cerebral palsy have spasticity, which is caused by damage to the motor cortex or   12._____

   A.   pyramidal tracts   B.   midbrain
   C.   cerebellum   D.   basal ganglia
   E.   parietal lobe

13. _____ problems are often the FIRST signs of cerebral palsy.   13.____

    A. Visual   B. Feeding
    C. Visual perception   D. Auditory
    E. Speech

14. Evaluation of a child for occupational therapy should include   14.____

    A. handling   B. positioning
    C. dressing   D. feeding
    E. all of the above

15. The role of an occupational therapist in neurodevelopmental treatment for children with   15.____
cerebral palsy emphasizes

    A. upper body control and acquisition of hand skills for self-care
    B. academic activities
    C. ability to take part in leisure activities
    D. ability to take part in community activities
    E. all of the above

16. Sensory integration therapy is a treatment approach developed by occupational thera-   16.____
pists for patients with cerebral palsy.
All of the following are basic principles of this approach EXCEPT

    A. to normalize sensory input
    B. to consider development in terms of the stability/ mobility spiral process
    C. to determine effectiveness by the child's response
    D. requires child and environment as a unit
    E. requires child to be an active participant

17. During the neurodevelopmental treatment approach for patients with cerebral palsy, the   17.____
occupational therapist works on head and trunk control to prepare the child for

    A. oral motor skills   B. fine motor skills
    C. gross motor skills   D. cognitive skills
    E. walking

18. The occupational therapist can facilitate upper extremity function by   18.____

    A. helping the child maintain proper alignment and relationship to the center of gravity
    B. guiding the speed and excursion of the movement
    C. inhibiting inefficient patterns
    D. reinforcing the child's improved movement verbally and reducing support
    E. all of the above

19. All of the following are benefits of proper seating and positioning for a patient with cere-   19.____
bral palsy EXCEPT that it

    A. decreases abnormal neurologic influences on the body
    B. manages pressure to prevent potential for decubitus ulcers
    C. decreases fatigue
    D. provides maximum function with minimum pathology
    E. none of the above

20. Persistence of the _____ reflex does NOT affect feeding. 20.____

    A. asymmetric tonic neck   B. symmetric tonic neck
    C. tonic labyrinthine   D. moro
    E. oral motor

21. Major treatment approaches for a child with cerebral palsy and drooling include 21.____

    A. oral motor therapy   B. behavior modification
    C. medication   D. surgery
    E. all of the above

22. A PRIMARY occupation of childhood is play, which involves 22.____

    A. exploration   B. experimentation
    C. imitation   D. repetition
    E. all of the above

23. Play deprivation is common in children with physical disabilities because of all of the fol- 23.____
lowing barriers EXCEPT

    A. limitations imposed by caregivers
    B. physical limitations of the child
    C. child has lost the desire to play
    D. environmental barriers in home, school, and community
    E. social barriers due to limited interaction with nonhandicapped peers

24. Toys which are good for learning and pleasure should have all of the following elements 24.____
EXCEPT

    A. interesting and age-appropriate
    B. capable of being used in different ways
    C. not expensive
    D. able to arouse curiosity and provide new information
    E. simulating social interaction and fun

25. By integrating play within therapy sessions, the therapist can promote interaction with the 25.____
environment.
The occupational therapist's task analysis skills are used to continually adapt

    A. size, shape, and consistency of materials
    B. rules and procedures
    C. position of child and/or materials
    D. nature and degree of personal interaction
    E. all of the above

KEY (CORRECT ANSWERS)

1.	B		11.	C
2.	C		12.	A
3.	D		13.	B
4.	C		14.	E
5.	C		15.	E
6.	D		16.	D
7.	B		17.	B
8.	A		18.	E
9.	C		19.	E
10.	D		20.	D

21.	E
22.	E
23.	C
24.	C
25.	E

———

TEST 2

DIRECTIONS: Each question or incomplete statement is followed by several suggested answers or completions. Select the one that BEST answers the question or completes the statement. *PRINT THE LETTER OF THE CORRECT ANSWER IN THE SPACE AT THE RIGHT.*

1. Early intervention means a comprehensive, coordinated, community-based system for developmentally vulnerable or delayed young children from birth to _____ year(s) of age.

    A. 1   B. 2
    C. 3   D. 12
    E. none of the above

1.____

2. The age factor is a key point or center of emphasis because of all of the following EXCEPT:

    A. During prenatal and early childhood stages of life, the brain is experiencing rapid periods of development
    B. Increased myelinization in the nervous system occurs in the first year of life
    C. The brain of the child is capable of more adaptive recovery than that of an adult
    D. The brain is highly plastic in the early years
    E. None of the above

2.____

3. Early experience is very important to children's development because

    A. environmental stimulation is not needed for normal child development
    B. it alters the process of myelinization
    C. the brain is highly plastic during early childhood
    D. genetic components have no role in development
    E. it lays a foundation and affects later development

3.____

4. All of the following are reasons for early intervention for a child with developmental delay EXCEPT:

    A. The brain is highly plastic and has more potential for neuronal restructuring following a lesion
    B. The final wiring of the brain occurs after birth and is governed by early experience
    C. If an intervention is not done now, it can never be done
    D. The critical period of brain development extends from pregnancy to childhood
    E. None of the above

4.____

5. The one of the following recommendations that would NOT improve communication between the occupational therapist and the family of a developmentally delayed child is to

    A. articulate information clearly
    B. share knowledge in family's best learning style
    C. emphasize child's and family's strengths
    D. deliver information regardless of parents' emotional and cognitive readiness
    E. give information regarding test results and changes in child's progress and program

5.____

6. All of the following are true for childhood autism EXCEPT: 6._____

    A.   Incidence is about 4 in 10,000 births
    B.   More common in boys than in girls
    C.   More prevalent in fraternal twins
    D.   Almost 80% have EEG abnormality
    E.   Brain damage is a possible cause

7. Developmental characteristics of autism do NOT include   7._____

    A.   cognitive deficits
    B.   communication deficits
    C.   social and behavioral deficits
    D.   sensory processing disorders
    E.   none of the above

8. Occupational therapy assessment and treatment of autistic children is very difficult, as   8._____
   the therapist must rely on

    A.   informal play observation
    B.   parent-teacher questionnaire
    C.   sensory motor responses
    D.   functional capabilities
    E.   all of the above

9. All of the following are activities of daily life EXCEPT   9._____

    A.   eating   B.   reading   C.   grooming
    D.   toileting   E.   dressing

10. The Brazelton behavioral assessment scale is used by a therapist to evaluate   10._____

    A.   a child's development in relation to other children of the same age
    B.   children who need early referrals
    C.   a neonate's reaction to stimuli and responses to the environment
    D.   manual dexterity
    E.   all of the above

11. The Brigance screen developmental test identifies children who   11._____

    A.   need referrals to special services and those who need further assessment for pro-
        gram planning
    B.   are normal
    C.   are not doing well in 5th grade
    D.   are deaf and blind
    E.   are autistic

12. The BEST test for individual assessment of deaf, blind, and multihandicapped children is   12._____
   the

    A.   Brigance screen
    B.   Callier-Azusa scale
    C.   Denver development test
    D.   Gesell developmental test
    E.   Bayley scale

13. The Bayley scale of infant development is used by a therapist to evaluate an infant's   13.____
development in relation to

    A. other infants of the same age
    B. other children of different ages
    C. the behavior of other children
    D. responses to the environment
    E. all of the above

14. The Bayley scales of infant development assess all of the following in an infant EXCEPT   14.____
_____ function.

    A. mental   B. motor
    C. behavioral   D. sensory
    E. none of the above

15. The BEST screening tool for detecting infants and children with developmental delays is   15.____
the

    A. Callier-Azusa scale
    B. Denver developmental test
    C. Brigance screen
    D. box and block test
    E. Gesell developmental test

16. The Denver developmental screening test is a tool to detect infants and children with   16.____

    A. mental retardation   B. abnormal behavior
    C. developmental delay   D. sensorimotor problems
    E. all of the above

17. The Gesell development test is used to determine mental growth for school readiness   17.____
based on

    A. developmental observation by age level
    B. sensorimotor function by age level
    C. scale of behavioral observation by age level
    D. IQ level
    E. none of the above

18. Which of the following tests uses 24 geometric forms, arranged in order of increasing dif-   18.____
ficulty, which are copied into a test booklet?

    A. Imitation of gestures
    B. Spatial ability test
    C. Perceptual forms test
    D. Marianne Frostig developmental test
    E. Developmental test of visual-motor integration

19. The Marianne Frostig developmental test of visual perception is used with _____ chil-   19.____
dren.

    A. preschool
    B. preschool and early elementary school
    C. early elementary school

D. high school
E. all of the above

20. All of the following tests used by therapists to assess sensory integration can be given to an individual and a group EXCEPT the

    A. developmental test of visual-motor integration
    B. Marianne Frostig developmental test of visual perception
    C. imitation of gestures
    D. perceptual forms test
    E. none of the above

20.____

21. It is NOT true that the Illinois test of psycholinguistic abilities (ITPA)

    A. is an individual test of cognitive functioning
    B. is used to assist in diagnosing learning problems
    C. can be tested in a group situation
    D. is a test of language perception and short-term memory abilities
    E. none of the above

21.____

22. A therapist can use the _____ to assess conceptual and intellectual maturity.

    A. Goodman Harris drawing test
    B. Peabody picture vocabulary test
    C. Bender-Gestalt test
    D. Minnesota multiphasic personality inventory
    E. Denver developmental test

22.____

23. The adaptive behavior scale test is used by therapists to assess

    A. verbal intelligence
    B. conceptual maturity
    C. cognitive performance
    D. adaptive behavior of the mentally retarded and emotionally maladjusted
    E. reading comprehension

23.____

24. The Bender-Gestalt test may be used by a therapist to evaluate

    A. intelligence   B. personality dynamics
    C. mental retardation   D. adaptive behavior
    E. all of the above

24.____

25. The nurse's observation scale for inpatient evaluation is highly sensitive ward behavior that assesses the subject's

    A. status and change over time in behavior
    B. personality dynamics
    C. recovery from the disease
    D. cognitive functions
    E. all of the above

25.____

KEY (CORRECT ANSWERS)

1.	C		11.	A
2.	E		12.	B
3.	E		13.	A
4.	C		14.	D
5.	D		15.	B
6.	C		16.	C
7.	E		17.	C
8.	E		18.	E
9.	B		19.	B
10.	C		20.	C

21.	C
22.	A
23.	D
24.	B
25.	A

———

EXAMINATION SECTION
TEST 1

DIRECTIONS: Each question or incomplete statement is followed by several suggested answers or completions. Select the one that BEST answers the question or completes the statement. *PRINT THE LETTER OF THE CORRECT ANSWER IN THE SPACE AT THE RIGHT.*

1. The comprehensive evaluation of basic living skills evaluates all of the following groups of basic living skills EXCEPT

    A.   personal care of hygiene
    B.   caregiving abilities
    C.   performance of high level activities of daily living such as meal planning, preparation, and clean up; shopping; telephone and transportation use
    D.   reading, writing, understanding time, money management, and math ability

1.____

Questions 2-4.

DIRECTIONS: Questions 2 through 4 are to be answered on the basis of the following information.
Mr. Miller had a cerebrovascular accident and is now suffering from right-sided hemiplegia.

2. As an occupational therapist, what adaptive equipment would you recommend to Mr. Miller to stabilize objects?

    A.   Pot stabilizer   B.   Adapted jar opener
    C.   Rocker knife   D.   Whisk to mix food

2.____

3. One of the therapist's goals in Mr. Miller's case should be to allow for safe, one-handed performance.
You should recommend a(n)

    A.   adapted jar opener   B.   rocker knife
    C.   whisk to mix food   D.   all of the above

3.____

4. If Mr. Miller is also having trouble with balancing, you would recommend that this task be done in a _____ position.

    A.   standing   B.   sitting   C.   supine   D.   rocking

4.____

5. All of the following are adaptive equipment which can be used for clean-up in a patient with hemiplegia EXCEPT

    A.   hand-held spray for rinsing dishes
    B.   rubber mat at the bottom of sink to reduce breakage
    C.   adapted jar opener
    D.   suction-type brush to clean glassware

5.____

6. Housecleaning tasks for a hemiplegic patient could become EASIER with the use of

    A.   a tank-type vacuum, permitting the client to sit and reach areas to be cleaned
    B.   self-wringing mop

6.____

C.   long-handled dustpan and brush
D.   all of the above

7.   One-sided upper extremity impairment can be caused by   7._____

A.   hemiplegia
B.   unilateral trauma or amputation
C.   a temporary condition, such as burns
D.   all of the above

8.   Reduced upper extremity range of motion and strength can be caused by all of the fol-   8._____
lowing EXCEPT

A.   quadriplegia
B.   multiple sclerosis
C.   first degree burns of the extremity
D.   amyotrophic lateral sclerosis

Questions 9-12.

DIRECTIONS: Questions 9 through 12 are to be answered on the basis of the following information.
Mrs. Rodriguez is suffering from multiple sclerosis, and now has decreased range of
motion and strength in her upper extremities.

9.   All of the following would be rationale for using compensatory strategies EXCEPT to   9._____

A.   compensate for lack of grip or reach
B.   compensate for decreased balance
C.   stabilize objects for task completion
D.   compensate for tolerance for prolonged activity

10. What adaptive techniques would you suggest to Mrs. Rodriguez to help her safely and   10._____
successfully complete the task of meal preparation?

A.   Position electrical appliances within easy reach
B.   Work in a seated position to conserve energy
C.   Use teeth to open containers
D.   All of the above

11. All of the following adaptive equipment will help Mrs. Rodriguez take care of her 10   11._____
month-old baby EXCEPT

A.   feeding the child in an infant seat or propped up on pillows
B.   large clothing with easily handled closures
C.   high chair with one-handed tray release mechanism for feeding
D.   disposable diapers with tabs

12. Mrs. Rodriguez also has difficulties in coordination of her upper extremities.   12._____
All of the following adaptive equipment would facilitate the task of meal preparation
and clean-up EXCEPT

A.   heavy cookware, ironstone dishes to aid with distal stabilization
B.   rocker knife and whisk to mix food

26

C. weighted wrist cuffs
D. rubber mat at the bottom of the sink to cushion fall of dishes

13. Paid employment that is provided to people with severe disabilities is known as _____ employment.   13.____

    A. competitive   B. supported
    C. handicapped   D. coaching

14. According to federal guidelines for a program to be considered supported employment, it must meet all of the following criteria EXCEPT: 14.____

    A. Employment must average at least 20 hours per week over the course of employee's normal pay period
    B. A competitive wage may not be paid in accordance with fair labor standards
    C. The disabled employee must be able to have frequent daily interactions with non-disabled employees
    D. Ongoing support - both on and off the job site - must be provided to the worker and the employer for an indefinite period of time through the use of a job coach

15. Work programs particularly targeted toward students with special needs should include the option of   15.____

    A. regular vocational education
    B. adapted and special vocational education
    C. individual vocational training
    D. all of the above

16. The occupational therapist may act as a direct consultant to the vocational teacher by providing   16.____

    A. adaptive devices
    B. work simplification techniques
    C. task analysis
    D. all of the above

17. The area of work practice provides many opportunities for the occupational therapist. The occupational therapist does NOT provide the service of   17.____

    A. assessment in particular evaluation
    B. job placement
    C. facilitate work adjustment
    D. adaptive techniques or devices for patients requiring vocational education

18. Work adjustment services should include all of the following objectives EXCEPT   18.____

    A. job placement and guarantee for job security
    B. becoming self-reliant and accepting supervision
    C. relating effectively to coworkers and developing safety habits
    D. development of work tolerance and motivation to do productive work

19. The MOST significant feature of aging people in the arts is that   19.____

    A. they should never be retired
    B. they should be given some social role in the community

C. they are not required to stop abruptly and reverse their roles from active to passive
D. their choice of leisure should persist

20. The theory of *role continuity* in retirement planning is the process   20.____

    A. in which active participation continues forever
    B. where present roles continue as long as a person maintains good health
    C. whereby people's activities and roles are adequate preparation for what will be expected at the next stage
    D. of continuity of present job

21. All of the following are common causes of death among the elderly EXCEPT   21.____

    A. heart disease   B. rheumatic disease
    C. cancer   D. stroke

22. It is INCORRECT to say that leisure   22.____

    A. is not self-determined
    B. falls into free time
    C. is psychologically pleasant
    D. provides opportunities for recreation, personal growth, and service to others

23. All of the following are true regarding the values or benefits of play EXCEPT play   23.____

    A. contributes to development in giving children a sense of mastery over their own bodies and over the environment
    B. contributes to the development of sensory integration, physical abilities, cognitive skills, and interpersonal relationships
    C. is a medium through which children learn to express themselves and develop symbol formation
    D. does not follow a sequential developmental progression

24. The reasons for satisfaction with leisure include the opportunity to   24.____

    A. recreate oneself
    B. gain new strength or to maintain good health
    C. provide variety, self-actualization, self-reflection, and contemplation
    D. all of the above

25. All of the following are functions of leisure related to a context that can also apply to work or play EXCEPT   25.____

    A. activity done for financial benefit
    B. enhancement of one's performance by improving skills
    C. prevention of idleness and antisocial activity
    D. socialization of the young into society

KEY (CORRECT ANSWERS)

1.	B		11.	C
2.	A		12.	B
3.	D		13.	B
4.	B		14.	B
5.	C		15.	D
6.	D		16.	D
7.	D		17.	B
8.	C		18.	A
9.	C		19.	C
10.	D		20.	C

21.	B
22.	A
23.	D
24.	D
25.	A

———

TEST 2

DIRECTIONS: Each question or incomplete statement is followed by several suggested answers or completions. Select the one that BEST answers the question or completes the statement. *PRINT THE LETTER OF THE CORRECT ANSWER IN THE SPACE AT THE RIGHT.*

1. All of the following are characteristics of leisure activities or experiences EXCEPT   1.____

   A. a sense of separation from the everyday world and a sense of timelessness
   B. freedom of choice in one's actions
   C. uncertainty
   D. a sense of adventure and exploration

2. All of the following are types of roles seen in group play EXCEPT   2.____

   A. functional: doctor
   B. relational: mother and baby
   C. character: Superman
   D. peripheral roles without any identity

3. Adolescents are developing autonomy and becoming socialized into the adult role. This is a period of transition affected by all of the following EXCEPT   3.____

   A. obligation and family and peer pressure
   B. academic pressure at college
   C. changes and refinements of interest
   D. time available for leisure

4. The single LARGEST activity of adolescents is   4.____

   A. socializing   B. television watching
   C. sports   D. reading

5. The adult's predominant use of time is in work and raising a family. Multiple factors affect leisure patterns in adulthood, including   5.____

   A. age and sex
   B. marital status
   C. whether one has children and children's ages
   D. all of the above

6. Older adults are thought of as having a great deal of leisure time. The MOST common activity for this age group is   6.____

   A. television watching
   B. socializing
   C. making small handicrafts
   D. reading

7. A therapist would know all of the following information about children by watching them play EXCEPT   7.____

   A. physical and cognitive abilities
   B. social participation, imagination, and independence

    C.   reading abilities
    D.   coping mechanisms and their environment

8. In occupational therapy, the focus of therapy with a child is on   8.____

    A.   cognitive functions
    B.   whole child functioning within the environment
    C.   motor functions
    D.   interpersonal skills

9. Which of the following statements is TRUE about the role of play in children's lives?   9.____

    A.   Play is an automatic and integral part of their existence.
    B.   All children engage in some form of play.
    C.   Play is an important treatment media in occupational therapy because of its importance to the child.
    D.   All of the above

10. The exploratory drive of curiosity underlies play behavior.   10.____
     This drive has all of the following hierarchical stages EXCEPT

    A.   exploration   B.   competency
    C.   boredom   D.   achievement

11. Exploratory behavior is seen MOSTLY in   11.____

    A.   neonates   B.   infants
    C.   early childhood   D.   late childhood

12. Competency behavior, a stage of the exploratory drive of curiosity, is NOT characterized   12.____
    by

    A.   fueled by effectance motivation
    B.   experimentation
    C.   practice to achieve mastery
    D.   none of the above

13. Play is also valued as the arena through which sensory integration develops. In therapy,   13.____
    the therapist sets up and manipulates the environment.
    The therapist adjusts all of the following to bring about successful adaptation EXCEPT

    A.   environment   B.   child
    C.   activity   D.   time

14. In the differentiation of free play from therapeutic play, free play is   14.____

    A.   intrinsically motivated
    B.   fun
    C.   performed for its own sake rather than having a purpose
    D.   all of the above

15. Therapeutic play offers a practical vehicle to enlist all of the following EXCEPT   15.____

    A.   ability to practice motor and functional skills
    B.   intelligence quotient

C. sensory processing, perceptual abilities, and cognitive development
D. support of social, emotional, and language development

16. The therapist's use of self is critical to engaging the patient in occupational therapy.   16._____
Of the following, only _____ is NOT essential to establish a therapeutic relationship.

    A. understanding   B. neutrality
    C. sympathy   D. caring

17. When the therapist feels the other person's condition as if it were his or her own, it means   17._____
that person is experiencing

    A. sympathy   B. empathy
    C. ignorance   D. personality crisis

18. When the patient experiences the therapist's respect and regards as well as an appreci-   18._____
ation of the patient's uniqueness and capabilities, it means that the therapist has developed

    A. sympathy   B. empathy
    C. therapeutic rapport   D. confidence

19. When terminating a long-term and intense relationship with a patient, as in a case of   19._____
going on vacation, the therapist should be aware of feelings of

    A. anger   B. sadness
    C. loss   D. all of the above

20. All of the following are characteristic functions of humor in occupational therapy EXCEPT   20._____

    A. maintaining the therapeutic alliance
    B. discussing pain most of the time
    C. correcting performance or reinforcing progress
    D. helping patient envision a life beyond the sick role

21. The technique of _____ is generally NOT used in occupational therapy.   21._____

    A. reading sessions
    B. feelings-oriented discussions
    C. arts and crafts
    D. exercise

22. To enhance the group process through group structure, all of the following factors should   22._____
be considered in planning, running, and reviewing the group EXCEPT

    A. maximum involvement through group-centered action
    B. a maximum sense of individual and group identity
    C. discouragement of spontaneous involvement of members
    D. member support and feedback

23. Mosey's classification of group interaction skills is OFTEN used to designate the   23._____

    A. here-and-now experience
    B. there-and-then experience
    C. type and level of interaction required in an activity group
    D. role of a parallel group

24. In addition to the group as a whole, the leader in a group session observes each group member in relation to

    A. other members   B. the leader
    C. group tasks   D. all of the above

24.____

25. The observation of a group process is 6conducted at all of the following levels EXCEPT the

    A. group
    B. individual member in relation to the group
    C. individual, the group, and the leader in relation to a task or activity
    D. therapist

25.____

KEY (CORRECT ANSWERS)

1. C		11. C	
2. D		12. D	
3. B		13. D	
4. A		14. D	
5. D		15. B	
6. A		16. C	
7. C		17. B	
8. B		18. C	
9. D		19. D	
10. C		20. B	

21. A
22. C
23. C
24. D
25. D

33

EXAMINATION SECTION
TEST 1

DIRECTIONS: Each question or incomplete statement is followed by several suggested answers or completions. Select the one that BEST answers the question or completes the statement. *PRINT THE LETTER OF THE CORRECT ANSWER IN THE SPACE AT THE RIGHT.*

1. Activities are the core of occupational therapy and are characterized by all of the following EXCEPT that they should

    A. be goal-directed
    B. be adapted and gradable
    C. not necessarily reflect the client's involvement
    D. relate to the interests of the client

1.____

2. By becoming involved in leatherwork and cutting leather with shears, a client gains

    A. bilateral coordination   B. eye-hand coordination
    C. manual dexterity   D. all of the above

2.____

3. While a client is receiving occupational therapy, he gains the experience of using his aggressive energy by using

    A. a modelling design
    B. a hammer with a mallet
    C. modelling tools
    D. shears to cut leather

3.____

4. By performing an individual activity at the workplace, a client learns and gains all of the following EXCEPT

    A. independence   B. control
    C. organization   D. pride

4.____

5. The use of modelling tools with leatherwork will NOT provide a client with

    A. coping abilities   B. propioception
    C. kinesthetic perception   D. motor planning

5.____

6. Working in a ceramic factory, a client is involved in repetition of positioning tiles. What will he gain from doing this activity?

    A. Organization   B. Coordination
    C. Endurance   D. Pride

6.____

7. A client needs to improve his hand strength. He is working in a ceramic factory. What activity would you recommend?

    A. Involvement with designing and coloring of tiles
    B. Cutting tiles to fit with a tile cutter
    C. Application of glue to tiles
    D. Repetition of positioning tiles

7.____

8. A client is involved in designing with color and sizes. The component that would be evaluated based on his performance is the _____ component.   8.____

    A. motor   B. cognitive
    C. social   D. sensory-perceptual

9. All of the following criteria assist in meeting physical restoration requirements EXCEPT   9.____

    A. provide action rather than position
    B. require repetition of the motion
    C. position in some cases
    D. permit gradation in the range of motion, resistance, and coordination

10. Which of the following should be used in the Rood approach for an inhibitory procedure?   10.____

    A. Hard touch   B. Ice packs
    C. Fast vibrations   D. Slow stroking

11. In the inhibitory procedure used by Rood, slow stroking is done for no more than   11.____

    A. 1 minute   B. half hour
    C. 3 minutes   D. 10 minutes

12. Depending upon the type of muscle tone and the developmental level of a person, a treatment program may be all of the following EXCEPT   12.____

    A. all inhibitory
    B. all facilitating
    C. inhibitory and facilitating
    D. transitory

13. A therapist is asked to arrange for activities of daily life for a person who has suffered an injury at the C4 level, causing quadriplegia.
The FIRST thing the therapist should recommend is   13.____

    A. a sophisticated environmental control system
    B. 24 hour nursing care
    C. home care
    D. institutionalization

14. An arm sling is commonly used to prevent subluxation of the shoulder caused by excess gravitational pull on weak muscles during ambulation and to   14.____

    A. give strength to muscles
    B. support flaccid areas
    C. facilitate supination and pronation
    D. facilitate abduction

15. Vibrators are used by occupational therapists when there is a need to stimulate   15.____

    A. motor nerve endings
    B. the sensory ending of the neuromuscular spindle
    C. secretions
    D. individual muscular response

Questions 16-20.

DIRECTIONS: In Questions 16 through 20, match the numbered muscle with the le6ttered
action, listed in the column below, for which it is responsible. (An answer may
be used more than once.)

            A.   Flexion
            B.   Extension
            C.   Pronation
            D.   Supination

16.   Brachialis   16._____

17.   Supinator   17._____

18.   Anconeus   18._____

19.   Tricep brachii   19._____

20.   Bicep brachii   20._____

Questions 21-25.

DIRECTIONS: In Questions 21 through 25, match each numbered muscle with its respective
lettered nerve, listed in the column below.

            A.   Median
            B.   Radial
            C.   Lateral pectoral
            D.   Axillary
            E.   Musculocutaneous
            F.   Medial pectoral
            G.   Ulnar
            H.   Suprascapular

21.   Pectoralis minor   21._____

22.   Supraspinatus   22._____

23.   Coracobrachialis   23._____

24.   Flexor carpi radialis   24._____

25.   Extensor pollicis brevis   25._____

KEY (CORRECT ANSWERS)

1.	C		11.	C
2.	D		12.	D
3.	B		13.	A
4.	C		14.	B
5.	A		15.	B
6.	C		16.	A
7.	B		17.	D
8.	D		18.	B
9.	C		19.	B
10.	D		20.	A/D

21. F
22. H
23. E
24. A
25. B

————

TEST 2

DIRECTIONS: Each question or incomplete statement is followed by several suggested
answers or completions. Select the one that BEST answers the question or
completes the statement. *PRINT THE LETTER OF THE CORRECT ANSWER
IN THE SPACE AT THE RIGHT.*

1. The purpose of the American Occupational Therapy Association, as stated in its incorpo-   1.____
    ration papers, is to

    A. act as a charitable and educational organization
    B. act as an advocate for occupational therapy in education, research, action, service,
        and standards
    C. establish an occupational therapy curriculum
    D. find jobs for disabled people

2. The American Occupational Therapy Association representative assembly is   2.____

    A. a group of members from each state who discuss occupational therapy concerns
    B. a forum for each state to share occupational therapy concerns
    C. the legislative and policy-making body of the Association
    D. the standards and enforcement body of the Association

3. The AOTA (American Occupational Therapy Association) representative assembly is   3.____
    presided over by the

    A. president of AOTA
    B. vice president of AOTA
    C. speaker of AOTA's representative assembly
    D. president of AOTA's representative assembly

4. The FIRST principle in the treatment of disabilities resulting from lower motor neuron   4.____
    lesion is the improvement of

    A. eye-hand coordination
    B. relieving muscle spasticity
    C. muscle strength
    D. range of motion

5. The MOST common cause of cerebrovascular accident is   5.____

    A. hemorrhage
    B. thrombosis
    C. embolism
    D. arteriovenous malformation

6. Which of the following diseases is congenital?   6.____

    A. Tetralogy of Fallot
    B. Diabetes mellitus
    C. Amyotrophic lateral sclerosis
    D. Multiple sclerosis

7. The incidence of emotional disturbance in patients with cerebral palsy is   7._____

    A. low   B. high
    C. rare   D. not determined

8. When cerebrospinal fluid exceeds clearance and spinal fluid drainage is blocked, it will result in   8._____

    A. hypotension   B. hemorrhage
    C. cerebrovascular accident   D. hydrocephalus

9. Hydrocephalus is the result of blockage of cerebrospinal fluid in the brain at the level of the _____.   9._____

    A. first   B. lateral   C. third   D. fourth

10. In planning for the development of strength of a specific individual muscle, the MOST appropriate method is   10._____

    A. testing the individual muscle
    B. testing a group of muscles and looking for specific motions
    C. observing ordinary activities and movement patterns that use the individual muscle
    D. using a functional muscle test including the specific muscle

11. An ADVANTAGE of using a splint to support a hand or a joint of a person with arthritis is that   11._____

    A. a static splint replaces the weak muscle
    B. a static splint substitutes for weak muscles
    C. it mobilizes the joint
    D. it counteracts the strong muscle group

12. Static splints have no moveable parts and, whenever possible, should hold the involved forearm and hand in a(n) _____ position.   12._____

    A. comfortable   B. abducted   C. functional   D. supinated

13. A static cock-up splint, when planned appropriately, may be beneficial in the restoration of upper extremity function, as it would support the weak wrist in a functional position   13._____

    A. at rest
    B. during activity of the entire extremity
    C. in the anatomical position
    D. both at rest and during activity of the entire upper extremity

14. A(n) _____ splint is MOST appropriate for strengthening palmar grasp, opposition, and prehension.   14._____

    A. orthokinetic   B. static cock-up
    C. static forearm hand   D. dynamic

15. The splint apt to do the MOST good in providing a combination of mobilization and support for relief of pain, increased muscle strength, range of motion, and muscle reeducation is a(n) _____ splint.   15._____

    A. orthokinetic   B. dynamic
    C. static forearm hand   D. static cock-up

Questions 16-20.

DIRECTIONS: In Questions 16 through 20, match the numbered surgical terms with their appropriate lettered definitions, listed in the column below.

    A.   Renal incision for removal of calculus
    B.   Plastic surgery of the ear
    C.   Excision of mastoid cells
    D.   Plastic surgery of the nose
    E.   Surgical creation of a gastric fistula through the abdominal wall
    F.   Removal of a lung
    G.   Incision of the colon

16.   Rhinoplasty   16._____

17.   Pneumonectomy   17._____

18.   Nephrolithotomy   18._____

19.   Gastrostomy   19._____

20.   Colostomy   20._____

Questions 21-25.

DIRECTIONS: In Questions 21 through 25, match the numbered stages of personality development with the correct chronological stage, listed in the column below.

STAGES

A.   First
B.   Second
C.   Third
D.   Fourth
E.   Fifth
F.   Sixth

21.   Phallic   21._____

22.   Adolescent   22._____

23.   Oral   23._____

24.   Latent   24._____

25.   Anal   25._____

KEY (CORRECT ANSWERS)

1.	B		11.	B
2.	C		12.	C
3.	C		13.	D
4.	C		14.	D
5.	B		15.	A
6.	A		16.	D
7.	B		17.	F
8.	D		18.	A
9.	D		19.	E
10.	A		20.	G

21.	C
22.	E
23.	A
24.	D
25.	B

EXAMINATION SECTION

TEST 1

DIRECTIONS: Each question or incomplete statement is followed by several suggested answers or completions. Select the one that BEST answers the question or completes the statement. *PRINT THE LETTER OF THE CORRECT ANSWER IN THE SPACE AT THE RIGHT.*

1. A short opponens splint immobilizing the thumb and allowing for prehension is usually indicated for
    A. low median nerve injury   B. CMC arthroplasty
    C. osteoarthritis   D. all of the above
                  1.____

2. Mr. S. complains his thumb is swollen and painful with motion. Examination reveals medial instability of the MP joint of the right thumb and a weak pinch. An occupational therapy referral for Mr. S. would request a
    A. dorsal long opponens splint   B. c-splint
    C. short opponens splint   D. gamekeeper's splint
                  2.____

3. A patient is referred to occupational therapy for a splint after sustaining a volar plate injury to the left long finger (LLF). A protective splint for this injury would be on the _____ of the LLF.
    A. dorsal surface   B. dorsal surface of the MP joint
    C. volar surface   D. volar surface of the PIP joint
                  3.____

4. The test that makes it possible to determine whether or not the radial and ulnar arteries are supplying the hand to their full capacities is the _____ test.
    A. Bunnel-Littler   B. Retinacular
    C. Allen   D. Phalens
                  4.____

5. Which tendons define the radial border of the snuffbox and are involved with Dequervaines syndrome?
    A. Abductor pollicis brevis and extensor pollicis brevis
    B. Abductor pollicis longus and extensor pollicis brevis
    C. Extensor carpi radialis and abductor pollicis longus
    D. Extensor carpi radialis and extensor pollicis brevis
                  5.____

6. The proximal carpal row of the wrist is composed of _____ and pisiform.
    A. scaphoid, lunate, triquetrium,   B. trapezium, lunate, triquetrium,
    C. trapezoid, lunate, triquetrium,   D. trapezoid, triquetrium, capitate,
                  6.____

7. To test for chronic shoulder dislocation, you would do the
    A. Yergason test   B. drop arm test
    C. apprehension test   D. scapular protraction
                  7.____

8. Upon muscle testing, if a patient can produce movement with gravity eliminated, but cannot function against gravity, then they have a measuring strength of
   A. good   B. fair   C. poor   D. trace

8.____

9. Mrs. D. has a nerve injury at the elbow region with loss of flexion of the PIP joints, loss of flexion of the DIP joints of the index and middle fingers, and loss of thumb motion. Which nerve has been injured?
   A. Ulnar
   C. Radial
   B. Median
   D. Anterior interrosseous

9.____

10. Which nerve, if severed, would produce a sensory alteration in the medial part of the hand, in the little finger, and in part of the ring finger?
    A. Ulnar
    C. Radial
    B. Median
    D. Anterior interrosseous

10.____

11. If a patient comes into the office with an inability to extend the wrist and presents with a wrist drop, what nerve has been injured?
    A. Ulnar
    C. Radial
    B. Median
    D. Anterior interrosseous

11.____

12. What injury is associated with a fall on the outstretched hand with the forearm pronated?
    A. Colles fracture
    C. Schaphoid fracture
    B. Sprained wrist
    D. Boxer's fracture

12.____

13. Street fighters who commonly fracture the distal end of the shaft of their metacarpal bone when they are punching with a clenched fist usually sustain what type of fracture?
    A. Colles fracture
    C. Boxer's fracture
    B. Schaphoid fracture
    D. Ulnar fracture

13.____

14. What kind of contracture is a progressive fibrosis of the palmar aponeurosis?
    A. PIP joint contracture
    C. MP joint contracture
    B. Dupuytrens contracture
    D. PIP and DIP joint contracture

14.____

15. Mr. R. goes to his M.D. after falling and injuring his small finger. He presents with an extensor lag of his IP joint, and x-rays reveal a non-union of his proximal phalanx. He would MOST likely benefit from what type of surgery?
    A. Extensor tenolysis
    C. Pinning of his PIP joint
    B. Flexor tenolysis
    D. No surgery at this time

15.____

16. Which technique is helpful in preventing post-traumatic edema?
    A. Elevation and early mobilization
    C. Use of cold
    B. Compressive bandaging
    D. All of the above

16.____

17. Which test does NOT fall under the category of sensibility functional testing?
    A. 2-point discrimination
    C. Touch localization
    B. Moberg pickup test
    D. Semmes-Weinstein

17.____

18. Which type of finger fracture has as its most common problem – following   18.____
a crush injury – pain and hypersensitivity?
    A. Middle phalanx fracture   B. Proximal phalanx fracture
    C. Diastal phalanx fracture   D. All of the above

19. Which type of fracture has been shown to be MOST common in 10- to   19.____
29-year-olds, with sports injuries as the leading cause?
    A. Middle phalanx fracture
    B. Proximal phalanx fracture
    C. Diastal phalanx fracture
    D. Both middle and proximal fractures

20. Which is the MOST common intra-articular fracture with an avulsion fracture   20.____
from the volar aspect of the first metacarpal base?
    A. Seymour fracture   B. Mallet injury
    C. Bennett's fracture   D. Rolando fracture

21. When categorizing levels of injury of flexor tendon repairs, which zone of   21.____
injury is referred to as "No Man's Land"?
    A. II   B. III   C. IV   D. V

22. Which symptoms are MOST commonly presented with a patient with carpal   22.____
tunnel syndrome?
    A. Pain
    B. Paresthesias more commonly at night
    C. Weakness
    D. All of the above

23. Which conservative technique is considered MOST effective when treating   23.____
trigger fingers?
    A. Operative management   B. Corticosteroid injection
    C. Splinting   D. Exercise

24. Which soft tissue tumor is MOST commonly seen in the hand?   24.____
    A. Ganglion cysts   B. Lipomas
    C. Xanthoma   D. Hemangioma

25. Which type of arthritis is the MOST common of all joint diseases?   25.____
    A. Rheumatoid   B. Osteoarthritis
    C. Lupus   D. Fibromyalgia

KEY (CORRECT ANSWERS)

1.	D		11.	C
2.	D		12.	A
3.	A		13.	C
4.	C		14.	B
5.	B		15.	A
6.	A		16.	D
7.	C		17.	D
8.	C		18.	C
9.	B		19.	D
10.	A		20.	C

21.	A
22.	D
23.	B
24.	A
25.	B

———

TEST 2

DIRECTIONS: Each question or incomplete statement is followed by several suggested answers or completions. Select the one that BEST answers the question or completes the statement. *PRINT THE LETTER OF THE CORRECT ANSWER IN THE SPACE AT THE RIGHT.*

1. Which nerve in the hand MOSTLY affects grip and pinch strength?   1.____
   A. Median   B. Ulnar
   C. Radial   D. Anterior interosseous

2. When there is a loss of wrist flexion strength in a median nerve related   2.____
   injury, the lesion is at
   A. wrist level   B. forearm level
   C. or proximal to the elbow   D. all of the above

3. The _____ nerve is the MOST commonly injured nerve in fractures of the   3.____
   upper extremity, being particularly susceptible to injury at the mid-humeral level.
   A. radial   B. median
   C. ulnar   D. anterior interosseous

4. What factor(s) affects prognosis for recovery after a nerve injury?   4.____
   A. Nature of injury   B. Motor versus sensory loss
   C. Age of person   D. All of the above

5. Following nerve repair, there is a latent period of how long after which axonal   5.____
   regeneration occurs at the rate of approximately 1 mm/day?
   A. 6 months   B. 3-4 weeks   C. 2 months   D. 1 year

6. Which sensory test is used to assess light touch to deep pressure?   6.____
   A. Pinprick
   B. Semmes-Weinstein pressure aesthesiometer
   C. Two-point discrimination
   D. Tinels

7. Which of the following activities is BEST to use for sensory re-education?   7.____
   A. Identification of textures
   B. Braille designs and finger mazes
   C. Picking up objects from a background medium
   D. All of the above

8. When doing flexor tendon repairs, which zone of the hand has poor results   8.____
   and has been referred to as "no mans land"?
   A. I   B. II   C. IV   D. V

9. Which exercises have been proven helpful in enhancing tendon excursion?   9.____
   A. EMG biofeedback   B. Blocking exercises for FDs/FDP
   C. Isolated blocking exercises   D. All of the above

10. Which tendon is commonly used to transfer when there is lack of opposition?   10.____
    A. Palmaris longis   B. Ring finger profundus
    C. Ring finger sublimes   D. Index finger extensor

11. Heat is transferred to tissue in which of the following forms?   11.____
    A. Conduction   B. Convection
    C. Convesion   D. All of the above

12. Which modality transfers heat via conduction?   12.____
    A. Hot packs   B. Fluidotherapy
    C. Ultrasound   D. All of the above

13. What therapeutic temperature is recommended when using paraffin?   13.____
    A. 105°F   B. 112°F   C. 118°F   D. 125°F

14. Which is NOT an effect when using ultrasound?   14.____
    A. Increased metabolic rate
    B. Decreased pain
    C. Assist in resolution of inflammation
    D. Increased superficial skin temperature

15. Which is the PRIMARY contraindication for using TENS?   15.____
    A. Cardiac pacemaker   B. Pregnancy
    C. Hyperirritable patient   D. All of the above

16. Splints may be used to   16.____
    A. prevent deformity
    B. correct deformity
    C. support, protect, or immobilize joints
    D. all of the above

17. Which test is NOT used to measure coordination?   17.____
    A. Jebson hand function   B. Purdue peg board
    C. Ninhydrin   D. Crawford

18. Which is NOT an indication for using functional electrical stimulation?   18.____
    A. Muscle strengthening
    B. Tissue healing
    C. Contraction correction
    D. Facilitation of voluntary movement

19. The _____ joint is the MOST commonly involved joint in the rheumatoid hand.   19.____
    A. MP   B. PIP   C. DIP   D. CMC

20. Which is the BEST method of increasing mobility?   20.____
    A. Heat   B. Passive mobilization
    C. Splinting   D. All of the above

21. Which diagnostic test is BEST for detailing soft tissue structures?   21.____
    A. Arthrography   B. MRI
    C. Computed tomography   D. X-ray

22. In which type of nerve injury does the prognosis for functional recovery   22.____
    remain good?
    A. Neuropraxia   B. Axonotmesis
    C. Neurometic   D. All of the above

23. The _____ joint is MOST commonly involved in osteoarthritis of the hand.   23.____
    A. PIP   B. DIP   C. MP   D. CMC

24. Which is NOT a symptom of trigger finger?   24.____
    A. Painful snapping
    B. Tenderness volary over the metacarpal head
    C. Disproportion between the flexor tendon and the A2 pulley
    D. Thickenking of the pulley and tendon

25. Which is NOT a cause of rotator cuff tear?   25.____
    A. Impingement syndrome
    B. Trapezium strain
    C. Thoracic outlet syndrome
    D. Anatomic changes as a result of trauma

KEY (CORRECT ANSWERS)

1.	B		11.	D
2.	C		12.	A
3.	A		13.	D
4.	D		14.	D
5.	B		15.	D
6.	C		16.	D
7.	D		17.	C
8.	B		18.	B
9.	B		19.	A
10.	C		20.	D

21.	B
22.	A
23.	B
24.	C
25.	B

EXAMINATION SECTION

TEST 1

DIRECTIONS: Each question or incomplete statement is followed by several suggested answers or completions. Select the one that BEST answers the question or completes the statement. *PRINT THE LETTER OF THE CORRECT ANSWER IN THE SPACE AT THE RIGHT.*

1. Of the following, the BEST source of trend information pertaining to occupational data is
   A. *The U.S. Industrial Outlook*
   B. *Estimates of Worker Trait Requirements*
   C. *Occupational Outlook Handbook*
   D. *Dictionary of Occupational Titles*

   1._____

2. Of non-white youngsters in the United States who drop out before completing four years of high school, what proportion come from families earning less than $20,000?
   A. 25%
   B. 40%
   C. More than 50%
   D. More than 90%

   2._____

3. Educational attainment has been rising. Median institution years of attainment for persons now holding clerical or sales jobs average
   A. more than 12 years
   B. less than 12 years
   C. more than 10 years
   D. less than 10 years

   3._____

4. Automation and technological development are causing job displacement throughout the economy. Which industry sector has suffered the most severe job losses due to these factors?
   A. Services
   B. Agriculture
   C. Manufacturing
   D. Professional, technical and managerial occupations

   4._____

5. *Choosing a Vocation*: Frank Parsons; *Mind That Found Itself*: _____
   A. Ralph Berdie
   B. Carl Rogers
   C. Mary L. Northway
   D. Clifford Beers

   5._____

6. The counselor will find which one of the books below extremely valuable
   in developing his occupational information program because it contains a
   complete annotated bibliography of career materials—books, pamphlets,
   posters, subscription services, etc.?
   A. Forrester, *Occupational Literature*
   B. Roe, *Psychology of Occupations*
   C. Greenleaf, *Occupations and Careers*
   D. Shartle, *Occupational Information*

6._____

7. The proper sequence of the four occupation categories listed below in
   accordance with the number of people employed in each, proceeding
   from highest to lowest, is
   A. manufacturing; government; wholesale and retail trade; services
   B. government; manufacturing; services; wholesale and retail trade
   C. services; wholesale and retail trade; manufacturing; government
   D. manufacturing; wholesale and retail trade; government; services

7._____

8. The vocational guidance movement, which is the parent of current
   guidance programs, was spearheaded by
   A. Frank Parsons
   B. Clifford Beers
   C. John Brewer
   D. Harry Kitson

8._____

9. Among the following occupational categories, the one expected to grow
   MOST rapidly in the next ten years is that of
   A. sales workers
   B. skilled workers
   C. managers
   D. clerical workers

9._____

10. The largest quantity of occupational information is published by
    A. Science Research Associates
    B. New York Life Insurance Company
    C. Chronicle Guidance Publications
    D. United States Government

10._____

11. The only occupational field – outside of farming – which has declined in
    actual numbers of employed since the end of World War II has been the
    field of
    A. printing trades
    B. tool and die machine work
    C. building construction
    D. unskilled jobs

11._____

12. One of the effects of automation and productivity has been to   12._____
    A. increase the education and training requirements of jobs
    B. eliminate many middlemen in trade and service fields
    C. decrease the number of semi-professional jobs
    D. lower the level of earnings in service jobs

13. Which of the following problems presents the MOST serious challenge to   13._____
    the counselor's skill?
    A. Redirecting the goals of the low-ability, high-aspiration students
    B. Redirecting the goals of the high-ability, low-aspiration students
    C. Changing the direction of a student whose goals are at an
       appropriate level, but wrongly directed
    D. Encouraging a client to investigate a promising field

14. There are a number of excellent resources for assistance in developing   14._____
    units on vocations. The writings of the specialists vary. Which of the
    following authors should you recommend on vocation?
    A. Gerald T. Kowitz
    B. Walter Lifton
    C. Robert Hoppock
    D. Gilbert Wrenn

15. Of the following occupational categories, the one that provides jobs to the   15._____
    largest number of people is
    A. craftsmen, foremen and kindred workers
    B. operatives and kindred workers
    C. professional, technical and kindred workers
    D. clerical and kindred workers

16. The *Dictionary of Occupational Titles* has developed a new coding   16._____
    system. Which of the following categories is NOT part of the code?
    A. Data   B. Ideas   C. People   D. Things

17. The most recent edition of the *Dictionary of Occupational Titles* includes   17._____
    all of the following EXCEPT
    A. the outlook for particular occupations in the next five to ten years
    B. bound volumes of occupational listings and descriptions
    C. occupations likely to be found in any industry
    D. training requirements and methods of entry into occupations

18. Most women who take jobs do so because of   18._____
    A. financial necessity
    B. desire to escape from boredom at home
    C. personal satisfaction
    D. desire to provide some extra luxuries for the home

19. The single largest employer of labor in this nation is which of the following
industry divisions?
    A. Manufacturing
    B. Government
    C. Wholesale and retail trade
    D. Construction

    19._____

20. High school seniors dropping out before graduation are MOST likely to
come from a household where the family head is which one of the
following?
    A. White-collar worker
    B. Manual service worker
    C. Farm worker
    D. Unemployed or not in labor force

    20._____

21. Of the following, the BEST source of fundamental information about job
situations and future trend is
    A. *The Occupation Index*
    B. *Occupational Outlook Handbook*
    C. *Dictionary of Occupational Titles*
    D. *Career Briefs*

    21._____

22. It was decided recently to screen all potential draftees far before
induction. The purpose of this step was to
    A. increase the number of volunteers
    B. get the unemployed off the streets
    C. get a better picture of the manpower skills available
    D. provide remedial help to people who fail the induction tests

    22._____

23. The employment picture in our country is in a state of rapid change. In
which one of the following states is employment increasing MOST
rapidly?
    A. Illinois   B. Oregon
    C. New York   D. Texas

    23._____

24. Of the following, which is the correct statement of a current occupational
trend?
    A. The geographic movement of workers is increasing
    B. The population is increasing, but the available labor force is
decreasing
    C. The proportion of workers aged 45 and over is decreasing
    D. The proportion of workers providing services is decreasing

    24._____

25. The manpower outlook in large cities in the years 1980 through 1990   25._____
    indicated a decline in the
    A.   number of persons in the resident labor force under age 25
    B.   number of semi-skilled jobs
    C.   number of females in the resident labor force
    D.   proportion of the population accounted for by non-whites

KEY (CORRECT ANSWERS)

1. C	11. D	21. B
2. C	12. A	22. D
3. A	13. A	23. D
4. B	14. C	24. A
5. D	15. B	25. B
6. A	16. B	
7. D	17. A	
8. A	18. A	
9. D	19. A	
10. D	20. D	

TEST 2

DIRECTIONS: Each question or incomplete statement is followed by several suggested answers or completions. Select the one that BEST answers the question or completes the statement. *PRINT THE LETTER OF THE CORRECT ANSWER IN THE SPACE AT THE RIGHT.*

1. The term "vocational development" is preferred to that of "vocational choice" by one of the following persons. He claims that in deciding on an occupation, one is choosing a means of implementing a self-concept; he claims, also, that the individual goes through various "life stages" in so doing. He is
   A. Ginzberg
   B. Axelrod
   C. Karnes
   D. Super

1._____

2. If present trends continue, what percentage of all workers in the U.S. will be women?
   A. 50%   B. 25%   C. 33%   D. 66%

2._____

3. Which one of the following occupational groups is MOST responsive to rises and falls in the business cycles?
   A. Professionals
   B. Craftsmen and foremen
   C. Semi-skilled workers
   D. Clerical workers

3._____

4. The more generally used forms of the *Kuder Preference Record—Occupational* contain nine or ten scales, each of which reflects an area or cluster of activity, such as mechanical, social service or clerical. The *Strong Vocational Interest Blank*, on the other hand, is typified by an approach which uses criterion groups of
   A. pre- and post-college individuals whose academic majors, interests and competencies are a clear matter of record
   B. successfully employed men in a variety of occupations whose responses are compared to a presumably representative group of men in general
   C. children at various social-class levels, whose interests and actual careers have been followed up subsequently for more than 25 years
   D. superior and marginal achievers in a large number of professions and sub-professions

4._____

5. Occupational information which specifies hiring standards is known as the
   A. job specification   B. job description
   C. job analysis   D. occupational analysis

5._____

6. State Employment Service interviewers classify experienced applicants according to
    A. the job opportunities available
    B. abilities and skills
    C. physical capacities
    D. educational background

6._____

7. Related jobs can more easily be located in the *Dictionary of Occupational Titles* in Part
    A. I   B. II   C. III   D. IV

7._____

8. Of the following broad areas of work in which people are engaged, the one in which MOST workers are employed is
    A. clerical work
    B. farming
    C. semi-skilled work
    D. selling

8._____

9. The proportion of the total working force engaged in certain broad occupational fields has shifted markedly in the period from 1910 to the present. Of the following, the field in which there has been the greatest increase is
    A. farm workers
    B. service workers
    C. laborers
    D. clerks and salespeople

9._____

10. Social Security or Old Age and Survivors Insurance is paid for by
    A. taxes deducted from the employee's salary only
    B. funds set aside by the federal government from income taxes
    C. the state in which the worker lives at the time of his retirement or death
    D. taxes deducted from the employee's salary plus an equal amount paid by the employer

10._____

11. If a counselor wishes to provide vocational guidance using as one basis an occupational-interest test, he must FIRST be certain the test has _____ validity.
    A. content
    B. predictive
    C. concurrent
    D. construct

11._____

12. Strong recently reported that a group of engineers responded to the Vocational Interest Inventory in the same manner as they had 20 years before. We may conclude from this that the test demonstrates adequate
    A. reliability
    B. validity
    C. usefulness
    D. efficiency

12._____

13. One of the major new emphases in vocational counseling which has been stressed by Gilbert Wrenn and others is that
    A. the counselor helps the student define goals, not merely to inventory capacities
    B. more women are going to be working in the future
    C. talent must be looked at in terms of its marketable value
    D. the counselor must stress the fact that satisfying occupations are decreasing

13._____

14. Unemployment has particularly affected the disadvantaged groups. For example, compared with a national average rate of about 6%, unemployment among teenage Puerto Ricans in New York City runs about
    A. 2%   B. 5%   C. 10%   D. 40%

14._____

15. Job mobility is an important factor in labor force dynamics. Which of the following groups has the highest proportion of persons who change their jobs in the course of a year?
    A. Unskilled laborers
    B. Clerical workers
    C. Professional and technical personnel
    D. Sales workers

15._____

16. In Menninger's view, which one of the following factors accounts for the greatest number of job dismissals?
    A. Technical incompetence
    B. Inability to relate to other workers
    C. Inability to relate to authority figures
    D. Poor work habits

16._____

17. Among American industries, there is much variation with regard to the unemployment experience of the workforce. Which one of the following major industry divisions generally has the highest unemployment rate?
    A. Agriculture
    B. Construction
    C. Trade
    D. Manufacturing

17._____

18. The only major industry division which is expected to decline in the next decade is
    A. mining
    B. agriculture
    C. manufacturing
    D. transportation and public utilities

18._____

19. The incidence of unemployment varies significantly by industry. The highest unemployment rates are found in which American industry division?
    A. Manufacturing
    B. Construction
    C. Trade
    D. Government

19._____

20. During the next ten years, job opportunities in government, in relation to total labor force growth, is expected to show the following change:
    A. more than average
    B. average
    C. less than average
    D. no change

20._____

21. Job opportunities are growing fastest in jobs requiring the most education; nevertheless, in 2000, what proportion of the labor force had NOT completed high school?
    A. More than 70 percent
    B. More than 50 percent
    C. More than 30 percent
    D. More than 10 percent

21._____

22. *Occupational Outlook Handbook* is a publication of the
    A. Vocational Advisory Service
    B. United States Bureau of Labor Statistics
    C. Welfare Council
    D. Vocational Counselors' Association

22._____

23. What is the general relationship of unemployment rates for non-white and white workers?
    A. Lower for non-whites
    B. About the same
    C. Twice as high for non-whites
    D. Five times as high for non-whites

23._____

24. Teenagers' unemployment experience, in relationship to the rest of the labor force, is evidenced in an unemployment rate which bears what relationship to the average for all groups?

    A. Three times as high
    B. Twice as high
    C. Fifty percent higher
    D. About the same

24._____

25. The highest unemployment rate experienced by any labor force category is found among which ONE of the following groups?

    A. Unskilled laborers
    B. Women
    C. High school dropouts
    D. Non-white teenage girls

25._____

KEY (CORRECT ANSWERS)

1. D	11. B	21. C
2. A	12. A	22. B
3. C	13. A	23. C
4. B	14. D	24. A
5. A	15. A	25. C
6. B	16. B	
7. B	17. B	
8. C	18. A	
9. D	19. B	
10. D	20. A	

EXAMINATION SECTION
TEST 1

DIRECTIONS: Each question or incomplete statement is followed by several suggested answers or completions. Select the one that BEST answers the question or completes the statement. *PRINT THE LETTER OF THE CORRECT ANSWER IN THE SPACE AT THE RIGHT.*

1. Of the following, the FIRST step in the vocational guidance of the physically handicapped is the determination of the subject's

   A. emotional and social attitudes
   B. previous employment history
   C. specific physical limitations
   D. none of the above

   1.____

2. Of the following, the type of job that might BEST be learned by on-the-job training, while receiving physical restoration and rehabilitation in a hospital, is

   A. medical stenography
   B. medical technology
   C. physical therapy
   D. telephone switchboard operation

   2.____

3. In considering broad areas of employment for many of the physically handicapped individuals, the group of occupations that should be explored for increasing employment opportunities at this time is the

   A. professional   B. service
   C. skilled   D. unskilled

   3.____

4. The group of occupations in which all the jobs involve the performance of simple duties, quickly learned and requiring little or no independent judgment, is the

   A. clerical   B. semi-skilled
   C. service   D. unskilled

   4.____

5. The *Dictionary of Occupational Titles* is published by the

   A. Psychological Corporation
   B. U.S. Department of Commerce
   C. U.S. Department of Health, Education and Welfare
   D. U.S. Department of Labor

   5.____

6. The number of job titles included in the *Dictionary of Occupational Titles* is APPROXIMATELY

   A. 10,000   B. 30,000   C. 60,000   D. 100,000

   6.____

7. The professional and managerial occupations in the *Dictionary of Occupational Titles* range from the occupational code 0-00.00 through

   A. 0-39.99   B. 0-99.99   C. 1-49.99   D. 1-89.99

   7.____

8. A rehabilitation counselor may be characterized as an assembler and interpreter of infor-   8._____
    mation which will aid individuals in making decisions.
    The one of the following which is LEAST likely to be considered one of his functions is

    A. constructing and administering tests designed to measure vocational aptitudes
    B. familiarizing himself with the physical condition of the patient
    C. securing and evaluating information concerning abilities, education, vocational
        training, and experience
    D. studying occupational information and comparing occupational requirements

9. Throughout the counseling procedure, the rehabilitation counselor should be in a posi-   9._____
    tion to discuss occupational information with the client.
    The one of the following which he would be LEAST likely to discuss in this process is

    A. interview procedures and techniques
    B. labor market information and trends
    C. nature of the work
    D. requirements and methods of entering the job

10. The counselor learns that a client had served in the U.S. Navy during World War II and   10._____
    has a detailed knowledge of fire control instruments aboard ship.
    One of the civilian occupations that should, therefore, be recommended for further
    exploration is

    A. accountant   B. draftsman
    C. medical technician   D. personnel man

11. The one of the following employments which the counselor should NOT recommend to   11._____
    an asthmatic patient is

    A. bank teller   B. heat treater
    C. statistical clerk   D. watch repairer

12. *The Fact Book on Manpower,* published by the Bureau of Labor Statistics, presents a   12._____

    A. guide on the physical demands of existing job titles
    B. series of tables and graphic information on the working population
    C. statistical analyses of manpower shortages and surpluses
    D. tabular and pictorial descriptions of jobs available for the handicapped

13. The intensive and direct method of obtaining the pertinent facts about jobs is referred to   13._____
    as job

    A. analysis   B. classification
    C. finding   D. none of the above

14. The literature in the field of occupations USUALLY classifies a group of tasks performed   14._____
    by one person as a(n)

    A. job   B. occupation
    C. position   D. none of the above

15. Of the following, the kind of information which has the LEAST relevancy in making a job   15._____
    analysis is

    A. economic   B. physical   C. social   D. technical

16. Of the following, the kind of test LEAST likely to be significant in determining achievement in the various trades is   16.____

    A. manipulation   B. performance
    C. picture   D. written

17. It has been the experience of rehabilitation counselors that failure on the job by a disabled worker is MOST likely to be caused by   17.____

    A. emotional maladjustment   B. insufficient intelligence
    C. lack of skills   D. physical incapacities

18. When a certain test measures certain qualities consistently, the test is said to be   18.____

    A. objective   B. reliable   C. subjective   D. valid

19. The point in a distribution of scores above which and below which lie an equal number of scores is USUALLY referred to as the   19.____

    A. mean   B. median
    C. mode   D. arithmetic average

20. That point on the normal distribution curve which is the greatest distance from the base line represents a measure of ability characterized as   20.____

    A. average   B. below average
    C. genius   D. superior

21. In statistics, the graphic representation of distributions from cumulative frequencies is called the   21.____

    A. frequency polygon   B. histogram
    C. ogive   D. parabolic curve

22. A frequency distribution is said to be *skewed* if the measures tend to   22.____

    A. be found at any point along a continuous linear scale
    B. be symmetrical, with one broad smooth hump in the middle, tapering off gradually at either end
    C. make a frequency curve in which the two halves of the figure coincide
    D. pile up at one end or the other of the range of measure

23. One measure of variability is the semi-interquartile range of Q.
This measure is half of the distance between which of the following percentile scores?   23.____

    A. 100th and 25th   B. 75th and 25th
    C. 75th and 50th   D. 50th and 25th

24. The standard deviation of a distribution may be defined as the   24.____

    A. percentiles of the total area which are included between the mean ordinate and the ordinates at sigma-distances from the mean
    B. square of the absolute amount of deviation from the mean that is exceeded by half of the measures in the distribution
    C. square root of the mean of the deviations from the mean
    D. square root of the mean of the squared deviations from the mean

25. As part of a vocational guidance program, a group of patients has been given two standardized tests.
If the relative rank of the patients is the same on both tests, the coefficient of correlation can be represented as   25.____

   A. .0   B. .50   C. 1.0   D. 2.0

_____

KEY (CORRECT ANSWERS)

1. C		11. B	
2. D		12. B	
3. B		13. A	
4. D		14. C	
5. D		15. C	
6. B		16. D	
7. B		17. A	
8. A		18. B	
9. A		19. B	
10. B		20. A	

21. C
22. D
23. B
24. D
25. C

_____

TEST 2

DIRECTIONS: Each question or incomplete statement is followed by several suggested answers or completions. Select the one that BEST answers the question or completes the statement. *PRINT THE LETTER OF THE CORRECT ANSWER IN THE SPACE AT THE RIGHT.*

1. Of the following, the test which requires the use of apparatus is the   1.____

    A. Minnesota Paper Form Board
    B. Minnesota Spatial Relations Test
    C. Ohio State Psychological Test
    D. Woody McCall Arithmetic Test

2. Of the following, the test that should NOT be used with persons who are unable to speak or read English proficiently is   2.____

    A. Army Alpha - Revised   B. Army Beta
    C. Wechsler-Bellevue   D. none of the above

3. The Minnesota Clerical Test is a test of   3.____

    A. computation, spelling, coding, cancellation, and classification
    B. general mental ability, weighted in favor of the person who possesses office aptitudes or skills
    C. simple computations - additions, subtractions, multiplications, and divisions
    D. speed and accuracy in checking 200 pairs of numbers and 200 pairs of names

4. The Crawford Small Parts Dexterity Test measures   4.____

    A. coordinated manipulation with both hands
    B. fine eye-hand coordination
    C. hand and arm movement
    D. manipulation of wrenches and screwdrivers

5. In the Wechsler-Bellevue Intelligence Scale,   5.____

    A. all instructions to the child are given in pantomine
    B. five tests are verbal and five are nonverbal performance tests
    C. nonpictorial diagrams are used in a series-completion type of item
    D. verbal ability is separated from numerical ability

6. The Minnesota Multiphasic Personality Inventory is a diagnostic test measuring, in part,   6.____

    A. attitudes of pupils toward school
    B. family relations
    C. masculinity and femininity
    D. study skills

7. The Thematic Apperception Test is a   7.____

    A. measure of aptitude for the appreciation or production of art
    B. measure of interests and preferences in a variety of occupations
    C. reading test based on interpretation of difficult paragraphs
    D. set of thirty-one picture cards

8. A broad survey of the many established and experimental methods of appraising personality through projections elicited from the individual is contained in *Projective Techniques,* a book by 8.____

   A. John E. Bell
   C. Quinn McNemar
   B. Florence L. Goodenough
   D. Lewis M. Terman

9. The one of the following which is NOT a book written by Dr. Arnold Gesell and staff of the Yale Clinic of Child Development is 9.____

   A. INFANT AND CHILD IN THE CULTURE OF TODAY
   B. THE CHILD FROM FIVE TO TEN
   C. THE FIRST FIVE YEARS OF LIFE
   D. THE MEASUREMENT OF INTELLIGENCE OF INFANTS AND YOUNG CHILDREN

10. A basic book in the field of vocational guidance, discussing the relationship between interest, intelligence, and personality tests, with illustrations of how the three should be utilized in counseling was written by 10.____

   A. Roger M. Bellows
   C. Edwin K. Strong, Jr.
   B. David Rapaport
   D. Robert L. Thorndike

Questions 11-20.

DIRECTIONS: Column I lists the names of ten individuals who have been prominent in the field of rehabilitation. Each of them can be properly matched with one of the items listed in Column II. Write in the corresponding space at the right the letter in front of the item in Column II with which each name in Column I is MOST closely associated.

COLUMN I	COLUMN II	
11. Barker	A. American Heart Association	11.____
12. Carlson	B. American Rehabilitation Committee	12.____
13. DiMichael	C. Arthritis	13.____
14. Kessler	D. Blindness	14.____
15. Lowenfeld	E. Cerebral Palsy	15.____
16. Menninger	F. Facial Disfigurement	16.____
17. Rusk	G. Hard of Hearing	17.____
18. Seidenfeld	H. Havestraw Rehabilitation	18.____
19. Switzer	I. Infantile Paralysis	19.____
20. Whitehouse	J. Institute of Physical Medicine, Orange, New Jersey	20.____
	K. Institute for Crippled and Disabled	
	L. Just-One-Break Committee	
	M. Mentally Retarded	
	N. Mobility Incorporated	
	O. Multiple Sclerosis	
	P. N.Y.U. Bellevue Rehabilitation	
	Q. Office of Vocational Rehabilitation	
	R. Organ Inferiority	
	S. Psychiatric Aspects	
	T. Social Psychology of Adjustment	
	U. Tuberculosis	
	V. Woodrow Wilson Rehabilitation Center	
	W. Woody	

KEY (CORRECT ANSWERS)

1.	B	11.	T
2.	A	12.	E
3.	D	13.	M
4.	B	14.	J
5.	B	15.	D
6.	C	16.	S
7.	D	17.	P
8.	A	18.	I
9.	D	19.	Q
10.	C	20.	A

EXAMINATION SECTION
TEST 1

DIRECTIONS: Each question or incomplete statement is followed by several suggested answers or completions. Select the one that BEST answers the question or completes the statement. *PRINT THE LETTER OF THE CORRECT ANSWER IN THE SPACE AT THE RIGHT.*

1. Studies show that handicapped persons rehabilitated under the state-federal vocational rehabilitation program repay in Federal income taxes *alone* the Federal government's ENTIRE investment in their rehabilitation within _____ year(s).   1.____

    A. one   B. three   C. six   D. ten

2. It is estimated that the number of individuals added to those who need vocational rehabilitation services each year in the United States approximates   2.____

    A. 50,000   B. 250,000   C. 1,000,000   D. 25,000,000

3. National *Employ the Physically Handicapped Week* is USUALLY observed during the month of   3.____

    A. February   B. May   C. August   D. October

4. The one of the following of the Federal aid programs of public assistance which was MOST recently developed is aid to   4.____

    A. citizens over 65 years of age not covered by social security
    B. dependent children
    C. permanently and totally disabled individuals
    D. the blind

5. The one of the following providing placement services for the physically handicapped which restricts its activities to veterans is   5.____

    A. Federation Employment Service
    B. Fifty-two Association
    C. Just-One-Break Committee
    D. Vocational Advisory Service

6. The one of the following hospitals which does NOT have a full physical medicine and rehabilitation service with a complete rehabilitation *team* is   6.____

    A. Bellevue   B. Bird S. Coler
    C. Goldwater Memorial   D. James Ewing

7. Of the following programs of services to the physically handicapped, the one which is a division of the State Department of Education is   7.____

    A. Governor's Committee on Employment of the Physically Handicapped
    B. State Rehabilitation Hospital
    C. Vocational Rehabilitation
    D. Workmen's Compensation

8. The one of the following which constitutes the LARGEST professional group in the   8.____
National Rehabilitation Association is

    A. counselors   B. occupational therapists
    C. physical therapists   D. physicians

9. Three of the following conduct vocational training services for the handicapped.   9.____
The one which does NOT is

    A. Altro Workshops
    B. American Rehabilitation Committee
    C. The Institute of Physical Medicine and Rehabilitation
    D. The Lighthouse

10. The one of the following that has a sheltered workshop IN ADDITION TO its other reha-   10.____
bilitation facilities is

    A. Bellevue Hospital Physical Medicine and Rehabilitation Service
    B. Hospital for Special Surgery
    C. Institute of Physical Medicine and Rehabilitation
    D. Institute for the Crippled and Disabled

11. The one of the following agencies that does NOT provide direct services to the handi-   11.____
capped is the

    A. American Rehabilitation Committee
    B. Federation of the Handicapped
    C. Goodwill Rehabilitation Committee
    D. International Society for the Welfare of Cripples

12. Of the following agencies, the one which is PARTICULARLY known for its program of   12.____
rehabilitation for the tuberculous is the

    A. Altro Workshops
    B. Brooklyn Bureau of Social Service
    C. Federation of the Handicapped
    D. Goodwill Industries

13. Of the following agencies, the one which does NOT provide vocational counseling ser-   13.____
vices for the physically handicapped is the

    A. Bureau of Social Services
    B. Federation Employment Service
    C. Fountain House
    D. Just-One-Break Committee

14. The one of the following publications which would be LEAST likely to be of professional   14.____
interest to a rehabilitation counselor is

    A. COMEBACK
    B. JOURNAL OF REHABILITATION
    C. JOURNAL OF THE ASSOCIATION FOR PHYSICAL AND MENTAL REHABILITA-
        TION
    D. PERFORMANCE

15. Each municipal hospital which has a department of physical medicine and rehabilitation has a *rehabilitation team.*
The one of the following occupations which is NOT represented on that team is

    A. bracemaker   B. physiatrist
    C. psychologist   D. recreation leader

15.____

16. Of the following, the one which is NOT considered to be a medical center is

    A. Beekman-Downtown   B. Columbia-Presbyterian
    C. New York-Cornell   D. New York University-Bellevue

16.____

17. The National Institutes of Health are a part of the

    A. Kellogg Foundation   B. National Research Council
    C. Rockefeller Foundation   D. U.S.Public Health Service

17.____

18. Results of I.Q. tests are used as predictors of all of the following EXCEPT

    A. learning disabilities   B. educational achievement
    C. job performance   D. athletic ability

18.____

19. The index usually used to describe an individual's relative mental brightness is

    A. C.A.   B. E.Q.   C. I.Q.   D. M.A.

19.____

20. Of the following, the BEST criterion of an individual's normalcy is his

    A. educational goals   B. interpersonal relationships
    C. moral values   D. physical standards

20.____

21. The one of the following which has been greatly expanded by federal legislation is the

    A. counseling services for disabled veterans provided by the Veterans Administration
    B. federal-state vocational rehabilitation program
    C. rehabilitation training activities of the Children's Bureau
    D. selective placement activities of the various state employment services

21.____

22. The one of the following who would be LEAST likely to qualify for services under the federal-state vocational rehabilitation program is a

    A. college student paralyzed by poliomyelitis
    B. migratory worker stricken by multiple sclerosis
    C. self-employed man, fifty years of age, disabled by arthritis
    D. worker suffering from an amputation as a result of an industrial accident

22.____

23. Of the following, the present policy governing provision of medical services by the Veterans Administration to veterans with non-service connected disabilities is that

    A. if a veteran cannot afford to pay for medical care, and if a bed is available, he can receive in-patient care
    B. if a veteran cannot afford to pay for medical care, he can receive out-patient care
    C. in-patient care can be given only to those with tuberculosis
    D. out-patient care can be given only to those with psychiatric problems

23.____

24. In terms of vocational rehabilitation, the MOST important area of information which the counselor must know about the patient is his   24.____

    A. educational achievement
    B. expressed goal
    C. previous job experience
    D. type of military service discharge

25. The type of counseling MOST likely to benefit a patient who is still unable to accept his disability two years after injury has occurred is   25.____

    A. educational   B. personal   C. social   D. vocational

KEY (CORRECT ANSWERS)

1. B		11. D	
2. B		12. A	
3. D		13. C	
4. C		14. C	
5. B		15. A	
6. D		16. A	
7. C		17. D	
8. A		18. D	
9. C		19. C	
10. D		20. B	

21. B
22. B
23. A
24. B
25. B

TEST 2

DIRECTIONS: Each question or incomplete statement is followed by several suggested answers or completions. Select the one that BEST answers the question or completes the statement. *PRINT THE LETTER OF THE CORRECT ANSWER IN THE SPACE AT THE RIGHT.*

1. The development of objective criteria for measuring the physical capacities of patients is MOST difficult in cases of

    A. coronary heart disease
    B. multiple sclerosis
    C. poliomyelitis
    D. rheumatoid arthritis

    1.____

2. The prognosis for vocational rehabilitation is LEAST favorable in cases of

    A. amputation of both upper extremities
    B. diabetes
    C. hemiplegia
    D. muscular dystrophy

    2.____

3. The term used for a medical specialist in *physical medicine and rehabilitation* is

    A. orthopedist
    B. physiatrist
    C. physical therapist
    D. physiotherapist

    3.____

4. It is *generally* accepted that the sense through which people learn MOST readily is the

    A. auditory   B. kinesthetic   C. tactile   D. visual

    4.____

5. An obturator is FREQUENTLY used with persons afflicted with

    A. aphasia
    B. cleft palate
    C. lisping
    D. stuttering

    5.____

6. Visual acuity of *20/200 or less* is USUALLY interpreted as

    A. ability to discriminate between light and dark
    B. complete blindness
    C. remediable with glasses
    D. industrial blindness

    6.____

7. Of the following, the BEST means for testing hearing ability is the

    A. audiometer
    B. hearing aid
    C. medical examination of the ear
    D. watch tick test

    7.____

8. Recent studies indicate that adults suffering from a hearing loss, when compared to those with normal hearing, are *usually* MORE

    A. aggressive   B. intelligent   C. shy   D. stable

    8.____

9. The perception of one's own muscular movement is called

    A. cataplasia
    B. kinesthesia
    C. synesthesia
    D. none of the above

    9.____

10. The one of the following types of speech disorders which will *usually* respond to therapy   10.____
and retraining in the SHORTEST time is

    A. articulatory disorders   B. cleft palate speech
    C. post-laryngectomy speech   D. stuttering

11. As a result of medical care advances, there has been, within recent years, a lessening of   11.____
the need for rehabilitation counseling services in hospitals for patients with

    A. amputations   B. arthritis
    C. hemiplegia   D. tuberculosis

12. The one of the following conditions which is NOT characterized by an orthopedic involve-   12.____
ment is

    A. amputations   B. congenital club foot
    C. diabetes   D. scoliosis

13. The use of isonicotinic hydrazides in connection with other forms of therapy is a   13.____
RECENT development in the treatment of

    A. arthritis   B. cerebral palsy
    C. muscular dystrophy   D. tuberculosis

14. The one of the following diseases in which insulin is used as a method of medical control   14.____
and management is

    A. diabetes   B. epilepsy
    C. rheumatic fever   D. syphilis

15. The one of the following with which aphasia is MOST commonly associated is   15.____

    A. hemiplegia   B. monoplegia   C. paraplegia   D. quadraplegia

16. The kind of patient with which a rehabilitation counselor in a municipal hospital would   16.____
come into professional contact LEAST frequently is the

    A. geriatric   B. neurologic   C. orthopedic   D. psychiatric

17. In the development of the embryo, the month after which the central nervous system, ori-   17.____
gin of overt human behavior, is well under way is the

    A. second   B. fifth   C. seventh   D. ninth

18. Three of the following symptoms are frequently associated with multiple sclerosis.   18.____
The one which is NOT is

    A. metabolic disturbances   B. speech difficulties
    C. stumbling gait   D. visual disturbances

19. Of the following, the term which does NOT describe a type of cerebral palsy is   19.____

    A. amebiasis   B. ataxic   C. athetoid   D. spastic

20. Three of the following diseases are frequently progressive in the chronic stages.   20.____
The one which is NOT is

    A. multiple sclerosis   B. muscular dystrophy
    C. Parkinson's disease   D. poliomyelitis

21. Three of the following are diseases usually classified as chronic neurological diseases. 21.____
The one which does NOT fall into this category is

    A. cerebral palsy   B. multiple sclerosis
    C. muscular dystrophy   D. rheumatism

22. The one of the following books that should be of MOST interest to the cerebral palsied is 22.____

    A. BORN THAT WAY by Earl R. Carlson
    B. IT WAS NOT MY OWN IDEA by Robinson Pierce
    C. TRIUMPH CLEAR by Lorraine L. Beim
    D. WHO WALK ALONE by Perry Burgess

23. In general, the percentage of patients stricken with poliomyelitis who will be severely dis- 23.____
abled is *approximately*

    A. 20%   B. 45%   C. 75%   D. 90%

24. With the development of anticonvulsant drugs, the percentage of persons with epilepsy 24.____
whose seizures can now be completely controlled is *approximately*

    A. 10%   B. 33%   C. 50%   D. 75%

25. The one of the following diseases which affects the SMALLEST number of persons is 25.____

    A. arteriosclerosis   B. congenital heart disease
    C. hypertension   D. rheumatic fever

26. Recent advances in the research and treatment of epilepsy have resulted from the devel- 26.____
opment and widespread use of the

    A. electrocardiograph   B. electroencephalograph
    C. electromyograph   D. electronic microscope

27. The one of the following books that should be MOST interesting to parents of a congeni- 27.____
tal amputee is

    A. AND NOW TO LIVE AGAIN by Betsy Barton
    B. OUT ON A LIMB by Louise Baker
    C. THE CHILD WHO NEVER GREW by Pearl Buck
    D. TRIUMPH OF LOVE by Leona Bruckner

28. The one of the following responsible for the GREATEST number of patients in mental 28.____
hospitals is

    A. drug addiction   B. paresis
    C. schizophrenia   D. senile dementia

29. Of the following, the LEAST important factor in counseling a patient with a unilateral BK 29.____
amputation is

    A. diagnosis
    B. etiology
    C. site of amputation
    D. type of prosthetic device worn

30. One of the MOST comprehensive references on the psychological aspects of the physi-   30._____
cally disabled is that compiled by

    A. Bitner   B. Garrett   C. Kessler   D. Zohl

KEY (CORRECT ANSWERS)

1.	A	16.	D
2.	D	17.	A
3.	B	18.	A
4.	D	19.	A
5.	B	20.	D
6.	D	21.	D
7.	A	22.	A
8.	C	23.	A
9.	B	24.	C
10.	A	25.	B
11.	D	26.	B
12.	C	27.	D
13.	D	28.	C
14.	A	29.	D
15.	A	30.	B

EXAMINATION SECTION
TEST 1

DIRECTIONS: Each question or incomplete statement is followed by several suggested answers or completions. Select the one that BEST answers the question or completes the statement. *PRINT THE LETTER OF THE CORRECT ANSWER IN THE SPACE AT THE RIGHT.*

1. A fusion operation upon the spine is often undertaken to correct   1.____
   - A. pelvimetry
   - C. epiphysistis
   - B. paroxysm
   - D. scoliosis

2. The treatment program for slipped epiphysis is MOST similar to the program for   2.____
   - A. torticollis
   - C. polydactylism
   - B. Perthe's disease
   - D. nephrosis

3. In general, the GREATEST difficulty is encountered in attempting to attain an intellectual   3.____
   evaluation of children with
   - A. muscular dystrophy
   - C. rheumatic fever
   - B. cerebral palsy
   - D. spina bifida

4. A physically handicapped child is enclosed in a box which enables her to stand and work.   4.____
   The child probably suffers from
   - A. scoliosis
   - C. spina bifida
   - B. Perthe's disease
   - D. cerebral palsy

5. Which one of the following types of cerebral palsy is characterized by uncontrolled move-   5.____
   ments, facial contortions and drooling?
   - A. Ataxia
   - C. Athetosis
   - B. Spasticity
   - D. Rigidity

6. Which one of the following is classified as a fissure of the brain?   6.____
   - A. Maxillary plexuses
   - C. Visceral cleavage
   - B. Periphlebitis
   - D. Parieto-occipital sulcus

7. Paralysis of corresponding parts on two sides of the body is known as   7.____
   - A. diplegia
   - C. monoplegia
   - B. hemiplegia
   - D. hemiparesis

8. Muscular dystrophy is a condition in which   8.____

   - A. the cause is known
   - B. there is apparently no hereditary transmission
   - C. several members of the family are often affected in the same manner
   - D. the juvenile type is rarely found in boys

9. A cleft of the vertebral column with meningeal protrusion is characteristic of   9.____
   - A. Sprengel's deformity
   - C. coxa vara
   - B. scoliosis
   - D. spina bifida

10. In general, children suffering from epilepsy should receive   10.____

     A. no psychological help if their seizures are adequately controlled by medication
     B. intensive psychological help regardless of seizure control
     C. psychological help only in instances where neurosurgery is indicated
     D. some type of psychological help in the form of psychotherapy, guidance, or counseling

11. Which one of the following diseases may result in brain damage?   11.____

     A. Poliomyelitis   B. Lymphadenoma
     C. Spondylitis   D. Encephalitis

12. Which one of the following involves the degeneration of parts of the brain, or spinal   12.____
chord, or both?

     A. Schizophrenia   B. Spina bifida
     C. Multiple sclerosis   D. Pott's disease

13. Of the following, the disability with the BEST prognosis is   13.____

     A. Cooley's anemia   B. encephalitis
     C. hemophilia   D. slipped epiphyses

14. A child who has cerebral palsy has difficulty in keeping his paper on his desk. Which one   14.____
of the following materials should his physical therapist provide to help him?

     A. A thick piece of oak tag
     B. A paper weight
     C. Masking tape
     D. A set of tacks

15. Excessive accumulation of cerebrospinal fluid within the skull is usually characterized as   15.____

     A. meningitis   B. microcephaly
     C. macrocephaly   D. hydrocephaly

16. Cerebral palsy is a term applied to a group of conditions having in common   16.____

     A. hereditary malformation
     B. trouble communicating
     C. microcephalic appearance
     D. disorders of muscular control

17. ADJUSTMENT TO PHYSICAL HANDICAP AND ILLNESS was written by   17.____

     A. Gesell   B. Michael-Smith
     C. Barker and others   D. Jersild

18. "Self-education" of children, accompanied by special emphasis on the training of senses,   18.____
is MOST closely associated with

     A. Strauss   B. Cruickshank
     C. Montessori   D. Lehtinen

19. In the education of physically handicapped children, current theory favors stressing the child's   19.____

    A. special interests   B. motor abilities
    C. kinaesthetic sense   D. potentialities

20. The use of a board with holes and a rod as an adjunct to a teaching device suggests an adaptation of a(n)   20.____

    A. abacus   B. flannel board
    C. typewriter   D. marble board

21. Which one of the following would be MOST useful in therapy for a brain injured child who has a severe perceptual disorder?   21.____

    A. Bright pictures that tell a story
    B. Basal readers
    C. Educational games that teach addition and subtraction facts
    D. Three dimensional manipulative objects

22. In working with children with cerebral palsy who have problems in learning to read because of perceptual difficulties, the physical therapist should   22.____

    A. point to the words so that the child can follow the text more readily
    B. emphasize oral reading
    C. use a plain card to guide the child from line to line as he reads
    D. remove the neighboring children so that they offer no distractions

23. Research evidence indicates that handicapped pupils, as a group, show   23.____

    A. a higher incidence of below average intelligence than the normal
    B. an IQ distribution that is skewed towards the upper end of the scale
    C. a concentration of IQ's at both extremes
    D. an IQ distribution that approximates the normal

24. According to Strauss and Lehtinen, rote serial counting should be discouraged with the brain injured child because of his tendency toward   24.____

    A. perseveration   B. distractibility
    C. perceptual disturbances   D. hyperactivity

25. In general, children suffering from epilepsy should receive   25.____

    A. no psychological help, if their seizure are adequately controlled by medication
    B. intensive psychological help, regardless of seizure control
    C. psychological help only in instances where neuro-surgery is indicated
    D. some type of psychological help in the form of psychotherapy, guidance or counseling

KEY (CORRECT ANSWERS)

1.	D		11.	D
2.	B		12.	C
3.	B		13.	D
4.	D		14.	C
5.	C		15.	D
6.	D		16.	D
7.	A		17.	C
8.	C		18.	C
9.	D		19.	D
10.	D		20.	C

21. D
22. C
23. A
24. A
25. D

TEST 2

DIRECTIONS: Each question or incomplete statement is followed by several suggested answers or completions. Select the one that BEST answers the question or completes the statement. *PRINT THE LETTER OF THE CORRECT ANSWER IN THE SPACE AT THE RIGHT.*

1. Which one of the following diseases is always congenital?   1.____

   A. Cerebral palsy   B. Osteogenesis imperfecta
   C. Rheumatoid arthritis   D. Pericarditis

2. Of the following, which condition represents a disturbance of the neuro-muscular system   2.____
   frequently accompanied by perceptual difficulties?

   A. Perthe's disease   B. Cerebral palsy
   C. Spina bifida   D. Talipes

3. The following symptoms are noted in a group of children: enlargement of the calf mus-   3.____
   cles, difficulty in raising arms, afflicted shoulder and face muscles, waddling gait. The
   children are probably suffering from

   A. spina bifida   B. polio
   C. muscular dystrophy   D. Perthe's disease

4. Of the following diseases, which one is hereditary?   4.____

   A. Scoliosis   B. Osteomyelitis
   C. Hemophilia   D. Chorea

5. In which one of the following diseases is overweight frequently a concomitant?   5.____

   A. Pott's disease   B. Epilepsy
   C. Slipped epiphysis   D. Coxa Vara

6. Hyperactivity is most apt to be observed in children who have   6.____

   A. muscular dystrophy   B. brain damage
   C. ileitis   D. rheumatic fever

7. Three broad categories of physical disabilities - orthopedic, cardiac and chronic - are   7.____
   often used for convenience in classifying children in health conservation classes.
   The group below which best fits into the category of "chronic" is

   A. rheumatic fever, muscular dystrophy, kyphosis
   B. nephrosis, colitis, hepatitis
   C. Friedreich's ataxia, osteomyelitis, torticollis
   D. rickets, chorea, arthogryposis

8. Congenital malformation of the brain is often associated with   8.____

   A. hydrocephaly   B. myelitis
   C. varicella   D. lupus erythematosus

9. The use of an electroencephalogram usually proves most valuable in the diagnosis of   9.____

   A. epilepsy   B. osteoma
   C. lordosis   D. nephritis

10. Incontinence is most often an accompanying symptom of   10.____

    A. spina bifida   B. lordosis
    C. Friedreich's ataxia   D. Hodgkin's disease

11. A child with a positive EEG reading is likely to have   11.____

    A. asthma   B. rheumatic fever
    C. convulsive disorders   D. nephritis

12. Spasticity may reduce a child's ability to respond accurately to a therapist's questions   12.____
requiring

    A. use of the sense of touch
    B. recall of prior learning
    C. knowledge of subject matter
    D. familiarity with domestic routines

13. Of the following, which child is MOST apt to encounter difficulty in handling spatial rela-   13.____
tionships?

    A. The child with spina bifida
    B. The child with ulcerative colitis
    C. The child with Pott's disease
    D. The child with cerebral palsy

14. Which one of the following is characterized by involuntary, abnormal movements in the   14.____
extremities?

    A. Myositus   B. Rheumatic fever
    C. Athetosis   D. Scoliosis

15. Of the following, the disease that is believed to have strong psychosomatic implications   15.____
is

    A. colitis   B. diabetes
    C. anemia   D. hepatitis

16. Which one of the following is a congenital disease that involves the internal organs of the   16.____
body?

    A. Cystic fibrosis   B. Nephritis
    C. Tuberculosis   D. Synovitis

17. Of the following disabilities, the one MOST likely to require a body cast is   17.____

    A. muscular dystrophy   B. scoliosis
    C. esophagitis   D. torticollis

18. Which one of the following conditions is CORRECTLY paired with an associated disabil-   18.____
ity often found as a secondary defect?

    A. Cerebral palsy - hearing defect
    B. Chorea - visual defect
    C. Perthe's disease - speech defect
    D. Torticollis - poor coordination

19. In which one of the following pairs is it MOST difficult to arrive at a differential diagnosis?   19.____

    A. Encephalitis - meningitis
    B. Aphasia - brain damage
    C. Poliomyelitis - muscular dystrophy
    D. Hydrocephalia - microcephalia

20. Abnormal brain wave discharges are MOST characteristic of   20.____

    A. diabetes   B. epilepsy
    C. herpes   D. Hansen's disease

21. Most studies of children showing physical defects indicate that the incidence of defects is   21.____

    A. greater among intellectually disabled children than among normal children
    B. smaller among intellectually disabled children than among normal children
    C. about the same among intellectually disabled and normal children
    D. sometimes greater among intellectually disabled children and sometimes greater among normal children, depending upon the specific defect under study

22. Of the following, the one which does NOT represent a *major* problem for children who have physical handicaps is   22.____

    A. reduced capacity for affective relationships
    B. prolonged or frequent absence from home due to hospitalization
    C. differences in physical appearance from other children
    D. diminished opportunity for normal educational and recreational activities

23. In comparing physically handicapped children with physically normal children, it is correct to state that the physically handicapped child will usually be deprived MOST in which of these aspects of development?   23.____

    A. Social   B. Cultural
    C. Educational   D. Familial

24. The ability of physically handicapped individuals to cope satisfactorily with ridicule and other difficult situations   24.____

    A. depends largely on the attitudes of society toward the handicapped
    B. may be strengthened by special training in social techniques
    C. decreases as the handicapped individual matures
    D. is a function of the sex of the individual

25. Parents of physically handicapped youngsters often tend to overprotect their children. In most instances, this over-protection may be attributed to the parents'   25.____

    A. recognition of the child's greater need for protection
    B. projection of his own dependency needs on to the child
    C. unrecognized feelings of hostility and guilt toward the child
    D. wealth of affection which has too few outlets

KEY (CORRECT ANSWERS)

1.	B		11.	C
2.	B		12.	A
3.	C		13.	D
4.	C		14.	C
5.	C		15.	A
6.	B		16.	A
7.	B		17.	B
8.	A		18.	A
9.	A		19.	B
10.	A		20.	B

21.	A
22.	A
23.	A
24.	B
25.	C

———————

THERAPISTS

CAREER DESCRIPTIONS

CONTENTS

THERAPISTS
CAREER DESCRIPTIONS

The primary objective of therapy is helping individuals with physical, mental, or social handicaps to regain their capacity for self-help and independence. To meet this goal, different kinds of therapists are employed, each with special knowledge and skills which can be used in rehabilitation. For example, art, dance, and music therapists bring both artistic and therapeutic skills to their work and try to improve the mental and physical well-being of their patients. Dance and art techniques are used as nonverbal means of communication, and, along with music, are often useful in helping patients to resolve physical, emotional, and social problems. Horticultural therapists use gardening, an enjoyable and relaxing activity, for such purposes as training disabled or handicapped patients, evaluating the abilities of patients, or as a social activity for patients. Corrective therapists treat their patients by using medically prescribed exercises and activities. Physical therapists work with persons who are physically disabled by illness, accident or birth defects. They use exercise and such treatments as heat, cold and electricity to improve the patient's condition.

Occupational therapists help individuals with physical or emotional disabilities by teaching daily living skills or job skills. On the other hand, manual arts therapists use industrial arts such as graphics or wood and metalworking to rehabilitate their patients. Recreation therapists use sports, games, crafts, camping and hobbles as part of the rehabilitation of ill, disabled or handicapped persons. Athletic trainers care for and try to prevent injuries of individuals engaged in professional, amateur and school athletics.

Persons whose limbs are lost or disabled through injury, disease or birth defects require highly skilled and specialized services, provided by orthotists and prosthetists. Orthotists make and fit orthopedic braces while prosthetists make and fit artificial limbs.

Speech pathologists and audiologists work with children and adults who have speech, language or hearing impairments. Rehabilitation counselors help persons with physical, mental or social problems return to or begin a normal life by obtaining satisfactory work.

It is obvious that therapy and related activities offer a broad area for career exploration by interested individuals, and in the following pages each of the specializations mentioned briefly here is treated in greater detail.

I. Art Therapist
   Activity Therapist
   Art Psychotherapist
   Art Specialist

Expressing personal ideas through art and achieving some sense of well-being as a result is a very old concept. Pictures have been found scratched or painted on the cave walls of primitive man, and many ancient tools and objects were designed not only to be useful but also artistically pleasing. Exactly what made the cave dwellers and their ancestors draw the pictures or design the objects is not known, but it can be assumed that they must have received some sort of emotional satisfaction from creating them. This is the basis of art therapy which, simply stated, uses the concept of art as a device for non-verbal expression and communication. Art therapy attempts to resolve the individual's emotional conflicts and encourages personal growth and self-understanding.

The most practical application of art therapy has been with those suffering from mental disorders, mental retardation or other problems of social and psychological development, but innovative work has also been done on a variety of other problems. Art therapists confer with members of the medical health team to diagnose patients' problems. Combining art, education and insight, art therapists assess their patients' problems, strengths and weaknesses and determine a course of treatment best suited to accomplish specific treatment goals. Art therapists plan art activities, maintain and distribute supplies and materials, provide art instruction, and observe and record the various relationships that occur during therapy sessions. Emphasis is not placed on the quality of the product, but rather on the well-being of the patient. Art therapists often work as members of teams of other professionals and coordinate their activities with those of other therapists.

Art therapists work with people of all ages who have varying degrees of impairment or with normal populations in schools and growth centers. They may practice with individuals, groups and/or families in clinical, educational or rehabilitative settings which include private psychiatric hospitals and clinics, community health centers, geriatric centers, drug and alcohol clinics, nursing homes, halfway houses, prisons, public and private schools, and institutions for the emotionally disturbed, learning disabled, brain damaged, deaf, blind, physically handicapped, and multiply disabled. Many art therapists who work in clinics also teach art therapy in colleges or universities, and may do research in some aspect of therapy. However, the primary involvement of most art therapists is with clients in some type of clinical setting. Art therapists normally work a 40-hour week, although the hours and degree of responsibility vary with the setting. The facilities they work in are usually fully equipped with art materials, tables, chairs, art desks, and storage areas, and in general the working conditions are good.

Job Requirements

Entry into the field of art therapy at the professional level requires a master's degree or its equivalent in institutional training. Undergraduate work in the fine arts and the behavioral and social sciences is not only desirable but, in most instances, required for entry into the master's program. An undergraduate program specifically planned to lead to a degree in art therapy would be even more helpful. Training is offered at a number of schools, clinical facilities, and other institutions located throughout the United States.

Licensure is not required for art therapists unless they work in public schools. In such cases, they must be licensed in the State in which they plan to work. The American Art Therapy Association, Inc. has estab-

lished a national registry for art therapists, and to be accepted for registration with the association the applicant must meet certain experience and educational requirements. A master's degree in art therapy and 1 year of work experience will satisfy the requirements, but there are also several other ways in which the requirements may be met. Specific information on other methods of meeting registration standards can be obtained from the association. Registration is not always required for employment, but each year more employers are asking for this credential.

Opportunities

The employment outlook for qualified art therapists is favorable, and opportunities in this field are expected to grow.

There are no uniform paths of advancement for art therapists. Promotion may take many forms including assuming additional responsibility, administering an art therapy project, or moving into a specialty field such as special education, psychotherapy, or drug counseling. In most instances, promotions are based on experience and/or additional training.

For further information, contact: American Art Therapy Association

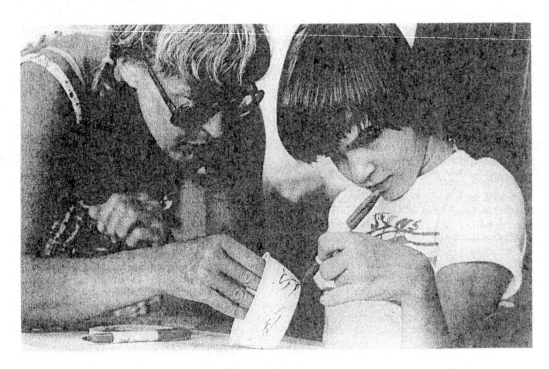

3

II. Athletic Trainer
Certified Athletic Trainer

Athletic trainers are professionally trained medical technicians who work in conjunction with and under the supervision of a physician. They are responsible for the prevention and care of injuries usually associated with competitive athletics. They administer immediate first aid to injured athletes and carry out treatment and rehabilitation procedures prescribed by the team physician. They also keep the team coach informed of the injured athletes' condition.

Trainers' duties include taking care of minor injuries such as cuts, scratches, abrasions, and blisters; making protective devices such as mouthpieces and injury pads; and taping, wrapping, and padding injuries. Trainers must be skilled in massage and corrective-exercise techniques and be able to use therapeutic equipment such as diathermy units, whirlpools, infrared lamps, and ultrasound machines. Athletic trainers also conduct conditioning and rehabilitation programs; plan menus and supervise diets; and aid in purchasing and fitting equipment. Some athletic trainers also make travel and menu arrangements for traveling teams. Since many athletic trainers are employed by educational institutions, including secondary and higher education facilities, they often teach classes in related or nonrelated subjects as part of their regular duties.

Most athletic trainers work in secondary schools, colleges, or universities, and a limited number are employed by professional athletic teams. The nature of the work requires athletic trainers to work long and irregular hours. It is not uncommon for trainers to work 55 or more hours per week. Emergencies and illnesses which require their attention may come up at any time, and the regular schedule includes any of the days and evenings of the week, often including holidays. Travel can be part of the job and is a necessity for trainers who work with a professional team, which may be away from home for long periods of time.

Job Requirements

The educational minimum for entry into this work is a bachelor's degree in athletic training, but an increasing number of candidates have graduate training. The certifying agency for programs in athletic training is the National Athletic Trainers Association (NATA). Typical courses of study include anatomy, physiology, physiology of exercise, kinesiology, physics, chemistry, psychology, first aid, safety, nutrition, administration of health and physical education programs, and techniques of athletic training. In addition, the program may lead to teaching certification in physical or health education.

Certification by the National Athletic Trainers Association (NATA) is not required to obtain employment, but it is considered to be a valuable credential in this field. To become a certified athletic trainer, an individual must meet a number of requirements, including having a college degree with specified courses and a teaching license. The certification candidate must also have worked for 2 years under a National Athletic Trainers Association (NATA) supervisor, have been a member of NATA for 1 year, and pass the NATA certification examination. There are colleges in 26 States which offer approved NATA curriculums.

Opportunities

At present, most opportunities exist in learning institutions. However, future demand in these positions may be determined to a large extent by federal legislation which, if introduced and passed, will require each school to employ an athletic trainer. Currently, the trainer with the best employment potential for these jobs is also able to teach a subject or subjects for which there is a demand. The more subjects the trainer is able to teach, the greater the chances for employment. Some athletic trainer positions require individual trainers to serve a group of schools or an entire school district. Under this arrangement, the trainer is usually located in a central place, such as a stadium, and has a small staff which provides the schools with an athletic trainer and facilities. In some cases, trainers take teaching positions in which they teach the skills of the profession to other athletic trainers. Competition is keenest for positions with professional athletic teams, and chances of starting a career as a professional trainer are very slim.

Advancement in this career is regulated by the employing institution or team, and, although there are no set patterns of advancement, a number of possibilities exist. One would be to start as an assistant athletic trainer, progress to trainer, and then to head trainer or director of training. A trainer at an educational institution might work into an athletic administration position. The athletic trainer whose employment is with a professional team is in a somewhat special employment situation. Usually, the professional trainer works only with one sport. Although most professional teams operate only approximately 6 months a year, they have an off-season program and employ the trainer during the full year.

For further information, contact: National Athletic Trainers Association

III. Corrective Therapist
Adapted physical educator
Therapeutic exercise specialist

Corrective therapists treat patients by using medically prescribed physical exercises and activities which strengthen and coordinate body functions and prevent muscular deterioration caused by inactivity due to illness. They apply the principles, tools, techniques, and psychology of medically oriented physical education to help persons with physical and mental problems meet their treatment goals. Therapists design or adjust equipment and devise exercises to meet the needs of patients. They instruct patients in proper exercise techniques and equipment usage to meet specific objectives such as walking, joint flexibility, endurance, strength, or emotional self-confidence and

security. For the physically handicapped, the exercise routines are aimed at developing strength, dexterity, and coordination of muscles. Therapists teach exercise routines to wheelchair patients, instruct amputees or partially paralyzed patients how to walk and move around, and sometimes give driving lessons to handicapped persons using specially equipped automobiles. They also advise patients on the use of braces, artificial limbs, and other devices. For the emotionally ill or mentally retarded, they use exercises to relieve frustration or tension, or to bring about social involvement.

Corrective therapists also judge strength, endurance, and self-care ability to gage the patient's recovery at successive stages. Corrective therapists participate in staff planning sessions and make ward rounds as members of health-care teams. They prepare progress reports on patient responses to therapeutic treatment exercises and present findings orally or in writing at staff meetings and conferences. Corrective therapists also counsel members of the patients' families on therapeutic matters. Corrective therapy should not be confused with physical therapy. Physical therapists employ physical agents such as heat, water, and light in treatment routines, and perform tests to determine nerve, muscle, and skin condition and reaction. Corrective therapy is used mainly in the more advanced stages of rehabilitation where functional training is required.

Some corrective therapists choose areas of specialization in this field. Corrective therapists who specialize in driver training are concerned with teaching handicapped persons safe driving methods, developing their remaining skills, and teaching them to use special driving devices. Seminars and workshops in driver training are required for this specialization and therapists working in this area are primarily employed by the Veterans Administration. Corrective therapists who specialize in cardiac rehabilitation are concerned with conducting programs of cardiorespiratory rehabilitation which entail checking patients pulmonary levels, establishing work performance limits, and establishing levels of progression to attain optimal fitness capabilities. Workers receive specialized training in cardiopulmonary theory, methodology and techniques, and the use of specialized equipment. Some corrective therapists are beginning to specialize in therapeutic exercise activities which are conducted in therapeutic pools in numerous hospital and health-education sites. This specialization requires water safety certifications, such as those given by the Red Cross or YMCA/ YWCA, and knowledge of effects of water activities and effects of water on exercise performance.

Corrective therapists work in a variety of government, public, and private facilities, including hospitals, rehabilitation clinics, schools, colleges, and universities, nursing homes, special schools, recreation facilities, and camps for the handicapped. They work a 40-hour week, usually in an indoor setting although outdoor recreation areas and pools

are also used. There are a variety of physical demands involved in being a corrective therapist, such as demonstrating exercises and equipment use, lifting and balancing patients, and handling and adjusting therapeutic-exercise equipment.

Job Requirements

A high school student considering a career in corrective therapy can plan on spending at least 4 years in obtaining a bachelor's degree in physical education from an accredited college or university. In addition to completing degree requirements, prospective corrective therapists must also complete a 400-hour clinical internship at an approved institution. Courses taken as part of the degree requirements, or in addition to them, include medical orientation courses in neurology, pathology, therapeutic exercise, developmental psychology, psychology of the exceptional/atypical, kinesiology,

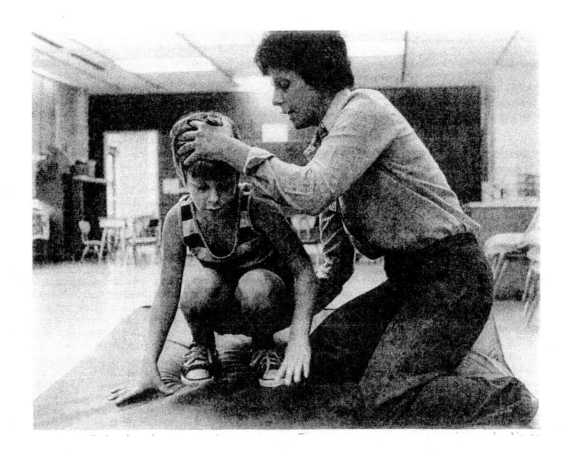

advanced anatomy, neuromuscular re-education, and physiological psychology. Many of these courses are required for a master's degree, and while this level of education is not required for entry into the field, it is considered an asset in seeking both entry level and promotional positions.

There are no State licensure requirements for corrective therapists at this time. However, therapists are eligible for certification if they meet the requirements set by the American Corrective Therapy Association. Requirements for certification include a bachelor's degree in physical education, specific medical/thereapeutic orientation courses, 400 hours of clinical training experience, and a satisfactory score on the certification examination. While certification is not normally considered a condition of employment, it is considered advantageous since it indicates that the therapist has met the standards set by the association.

The association also encourages its membership to enroll in continuing education courses as a means of improving professional growth and development.

Opportunities

The employment opportunities for corrective therapists are favorable. There is also the prospect of future growth and expansion in the profession as the importance of corrective therapists in rehabilitation is recognized to a greater degree and increases in government funding of programs occur.

Advancement to supervisory or administrative positions is possible for qualified therapists. Promotions are generally based on work experience, level of skill, and the completion of advanced education courses. Therapists in government facilities can advance through the traditional civil service methods.

For further information, contact: American Corrective Therapy Association

IV. Dance Therapist
Dance/movement therapist
Movement therapist
Psychomotor therapist

For centuries dancing and related types of body movement have been recognized and used not only as a form of entertainment but also as a way to ease tension and obtain other physical and emotional benefits. To many, this type of physical activity produces a renewal of emotional well-being, a means of self-expression, and a recharging of energy that has been drained away by the frustrations of everyday living. In this sense dancing and body movement are therapeutic activities. A practical application for use with individuals who have emotional and often physical impairments caused by injury, illness, or birth defects has been developed by dance therapists who use dance and body movement as a tool to further emotional and physical integration and well-being. They take advantage of the expressive and communicative aspects of dance to help people resolve social, emotional, and physical disorders.

Dance therapists make an assessment of their client's emotional and social behavior, movement capabilities, and general posture. They then determine what types of movement experiences will best help the client to develop an increased awareness of feelings and nonverbal behavior, a wider, closer interaction of mind and body, an improved body image, improved social relations, and relief from physical and emotional blocks. Working with individuals and groups, dance therapists plan and conduct movement sessions designed to achieve those goals and objectives that they have worked out with their clients. In many instances, dance therapists also work in cooperation with other mental health professionals. They discuss client goals and progress to coordinate treatment activities and work toward overall objectives. Dance therapists also participate in case conferences, staff meetings, community meetings, verbal therapy sessions, and other activities, depending on the setting in which they work.

Some engage in research on movement behavior, teach or train others in educational or employment settings, or act as consultants to various agencies or organizations. While there are many varieties of dance therapy settings, only one real area of specialization exists: movement research. The movement researcher observes, records, and analyzes nonverbal behavior in live settings, on videotape, or on film. In addition to the general knowledge and experience required of the dance therapist, the movement researcher must have completed advanced courses in movement observation and research methods.

Dance therapists work in a variety of mental-health settings, including psychiatric hospitals, clinics, day-care centers, community mental-health centers, developmental centers, correctional facilities, special schools, substance-abuse programs, and facilities for the aged. Registered dance therapists may also work in private practice or teach in educational facilities. Hours and other working conditions vary, as do the facilities themselves. Some are modern and well equipped, while others are older and sometimes quite sparse in terms of equipment and other things that contribute to pleasant work/therapy setting. Most aspects of the work involve close physical contact with different types of patient groups, as well as a good deal of physical activity. In all instances, strength, flexibility, stamina, and a strong desire to relate to and help others are necessary.

Job Requirements

There are two basic ways in which an individual may prepare for a career as a dance therapist. The first is the master's degree from a program in dance therapy, which is required for registry by the American Dance Therapy Association. The alternate way is a master's degree in a related field (e.g., psychology) with intensive training in the theory and practice of dance therapy and internship experience.

Neither method of preparation requires specific high school courses, but dance training in a broad range of techniques is strongly preferred. The minimum preprofessional training includes a B.S. or B.A. drgree with extensive training in a variety of dance forms, course work in psychology and other social sciences, anatomy, and kinesiology. The preferred pre-pro-fessional training includes a bachelor's degree in liberal arts with emphasis in dance or psychology, courses in dance theory, performing and choreographic experience, experience in teaching dance to normal populations, and experience in personal psychotherapy. Either program may require a movement interview for acceptance.

The master's program in dance therapy, which is from 1 1/2 to 2 years in length, includes training in both theoretical and practical aspects of dance therapy. Studies emphasize using body movement to establish communication and rapport with clients and learning to observe and analyze movement behavior. Courses include practical training and dance therapy, movement observation, psychodynamics, and studies in human behavior. Supervised experience in clinical settings, field visits, and internships are also included.

The possible alternate requires a master's degree in a related field (dance, psychology, social work, etc.), at least 120 hours each of theory and practice of dance therapy, and course work in group dynamics, anatomy and kinesiology, and techniques of observing and assessing movement behavior. A 700 hour clinical internship, supervised by a registered dance therapist, is also required. The disadvantage of this type of program is that it may lack the coherence and integration of a master's degree program in dance therapy. It is useful for those who already have a master's degree in a related field and can complete the other required course work before September 1983.

There are no licensing requirements for this work, and most employers do not require registration or certification. However, the American Dance Therapy Association (ADTA) has established a registry to insure professional standards of training and practice. Registration with this association is needed to work in private practice and to train dance therapy students. It may also be preferred by many employers, especially if there is a dance therapy internship program in existence at the facility or projected for the future, but there are no laws which require registration for employment. To qualify for registry with the ADTA at present, there are several requirements which must be met. Generally, they include membership in the ADTA; a bachelor's degree (a master's degree in 1980) with prescribed education, training, and experience requirements; 2 years of paid experience with work in several specific areas of dance therapy; and a written description of a therapy session showing an integration of dance therapy theory and practice.

Opportunities

At present, dance therapy jobs are in short supply, but several factors may influence this situation, including a growing interest in nonverbal communication; awareness of the importance of body image in mental health and education; and the maintenance of high training standards. If each of these factors remain constant or accelerate and money is available, demand for dance therapists in all areas should open up. However, interested individuals should check available openings in their areas and contact the professional association to get a detailed report of local labor market conditions.

In most cases, advancement possibilities in this field are determined by the requirements of the employing facility and standards and practices vary greatly. However, a master's degree and paid work experience are factors given heavy consideration for promotion to senior clinical positions in

most facilities. Teaching or administrative skills are also quite useful for purposes of advancement.

For further information, contact: American Dance Therapy Association

V. Horticultural Therapist
Garden therapist
Hort-therapist

Horticultural therapists use horticultural activities as the primary treatment method to bring about a beneficial change in an individual with a physical, mental, or social handicap. They use gardening for a variety of purposes, such as to rehabilitate patients after illness or injury; train impaired, disabled, and handicapped persons; evaluate patients' disabilities and capabilities; and provide a social activity for physically and mentally impaired persons.

Horticultural therapists organize indoor or outdoor programs for patients with different types of problems and usually do so in a group setting. They use plant materials to help handicapped individuals improve their emotional attitudes through a change in self-concept, their social skills through nonthreatening relations with others, their physical skills through activities requiring both gross and fine motor coordination, and their mental skills. Horticultural therapists work closely with other staff members to design and conduct the program suited to the needs of the particular client. In some programs, particularly those related to vocational rehabilitation, the plants may be sold, and in this situation the therapist may also have some business responsibilities. In addition to working directly with patients, horticultural therapists often teach at local colleges or universities and conduct workshops and other training programs.

Most horticultural therapists work in public or private facilities for the handicapped, including convalescent homes, juvenile centers, schools and training centers for the mentally retarded, psychiatric hospitals, tients in their work activities toward their rehabilitation goals.

Manual arts therapists prepare reports describing patients' emotional and social adjustment and physical performance and work tolerance. These reports are used by the rehabilitation team in judging the progress of patients and their ability to meet the physical and mental demands of their place in the community and in the world of work.

The majority of manual arts therapists are employed in hospitals and centers operated by the Veterans Administration, but they also work in sheltered workshops, mental health clinics, workmen's compensation rehabilitation centers and rehabilitation centers for the blind. The federal law requiring schooling for all handicapped children has opened a new field. Therapists normally work indoors from 8:00 AM to 4:30 PM 5 days a week, do little traveling, and generally have good working conditions. Because of the workshop setting, some noise, dust and fumes are normally present, but these factors are usually controlled.

Job Requirements

The minimum qualification for employment in this field is a bachelor's degree in industrial arts or manual arts therapy. In addition, candidates must complete clinical training lasting several months during which the student trainees work with fully qualified therapists and participate under supervision in a treatment program. Clinical training is usually given in hospitals or rehabilitation centers affiliated with colleges.

The American Association for Rehabilitation Therapy is the professional society for manual arts therapists and sponsors the Registry of Medical Rehabilitation Therapists and Specialists. The registry requires that a therapist be employed for 1 year in the field before being eligible for registration. Registry and membership in the association is not a condition for employment but both are considered desirable, because of opportunities for continuing education by attending seminars, meetings and conferences, and

pre-professional growth by exchange of information with other professionals.

Opportunities

The employment outlook for manual arts therapists is average, and with the current growth in rehabilitation, the demand for manual arts therapists is expected to increase slightly. The largest single employer is the Veterans Administration, with entry through the federal civil service system. Manual arts therapists may also be employed by State, local, and private facilities. Promotional opportunities in civil service are determined by specific rules; in private facilities they vary widely. Experience and competence are significant factors for promotion.

For further information, contact:
American Association for Rehabilitation Therapy

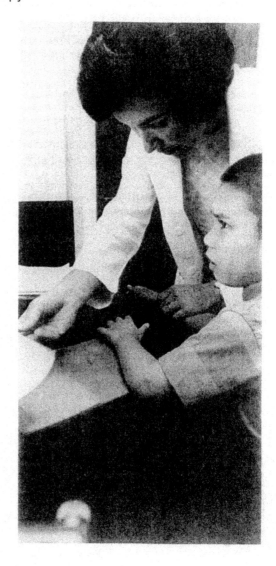

and general-care hospitals. Horticultural therapists work closely with both people and plants, and the work setting is often a greenhouse or outside garden. Care of plants can be demanding, and the ability to move the hands easily and skillfully is very important. However, there are no physical requirements for the job, and handicapped individuals may, in fact, have the advantage of serving as role-models for patients.

Job Requirements

Degrees in horticultural therapy are offered by colleges of agriculture and departments of horticulture and forestry in a number of universities. There are four levels of degrees in horticultural therapy; associate of arts, bachelor of science, master of science, and a doctorate. The length of training varies with the student's academic goal, which may be an associate degree leading to a position as a horticultural therapy aide or a bachelor of science degree which leads to a position as horticultural therapist. The training program consists of a horticulture curriculum with courses related to therapy as a specialization, plus internship and field studies.

At this time horticultural therapists are registered under a voluntary registration procedure administered by the National Council for Therapy and Rehabilitation through Horticulture. Neither registration nor continuing education is required at this time; however, all practitioners are strongly encouraged to participate.

Opportunities

Since this is a very new professional field, it is difficult to make accurate projections as to future occupational opportunities. However, the experience of the National Council for Therapy and Rehabilitation through Horticulture and a study conducted under the auspices of the Office of Education (HEW) indicate that the potential for jobs in this field is excellent and will continue to increase in the future.

Most horticultural therapy programs today are new and small, but they show signs of rapid growth. As programs increase in size, the opportunities for supervisory and other higher level positions are expected to expand. In addition, therapists who complete advanced training and education can obtain teaching positions in their field.

For further information, contact: National Council for Therapy and Rehabilitation through Horticulture

VI. Manual Arts Therapist
   Compensated-work therapist
   Incentive therapist
   Industrial therapist
   Recreation specialist
   Sheltered workshop supervisor
   Vocational therapist
   Work evaluator

Manual arts therapists use mechanical, technical, and industrial activities which are vocationally significant to assist patients in their recovery and in maintaining, improving, or developing work skills. Under the direction of a physician, manual arts therapists develop a program of actual or simulated work situations which help patients to prepare for an early return to their communities as well as to the world of work.

In rehabilitation, manual arts therapists apply clinical techniques for treating the physical or mental conditions of their patients, observe their behavior, assist in their adjustment to work situations, and evaluate their manual abilities and work skills. The primary purpose is to engage patients in therapeutic activities which absorb them and help in their recovery, giving them a sense of confidence and achievement. At the same time, these work activities have a practical value since they serve to retrain patients in their own skills or trades or, where disability makes this impossible, to help them explore and learn new work skills or avocational activities.

Manual arts therapists cooperate with all members of the rehabilitation team to plan and organize work activities, considering the patient's disabilities and capabilities. Manual arts therapy may be the only therapy prescribed for a patient, or it may be used together with other therapies in a combined treatment program. It may be prescribed at any stage in the hospitalization, depending on the patient's condition and rehabilitation goals.

Patients may explore various work activities offered in manual arts therapy, including woodworking, metal working, electronics, printing and graphic arts, and sometimes agriculture. For example, a construction worker who has lost a leg in a fall may discover an interest in drawing and be taught technical drafting. A bedridden patient may learn basic electricity by using batteries and simple hookups and later advance to electronics. A patient in a wheelchair mav explore jewelry or watch repair. A group of mental patients may help maintain hospital grounds. It is the job of the manual arts therapist to observe, evaluate, and guide the patient.

VII. Music Therapist
   Adjunctive therapist
   Creative arts therapist
   Music specialist
   Rehabilitation therapist
   Therapeutic activities worker

Music has been a part of almost every culture and is recognized everywhere as having healing value. A great deal has been written about its effects and it is often described as soothing, relaxing, exciting, moving, or in terms of some other emotional feeling it creates in the listener or performer. For each individual it serves a different purpose, and for some, many purposes. For those who are disabled, music may become an actual part of medical treatment.

Music therapists have an understanding of both music and psychology and are specialists in using music as a means of accomplishing treatment goals which involve the restoration, maintenance, and improvement of mental and physical health.

In its use with the mentally ill, music therapy may achieve changes in patients' behavior that will give them new understanding of themselves and of the world around them. This can serve as a basis for improved mental health and more effective adjustment to normal living.

Often working as members of a team that may include other therapists, psychiatrists, psychologists, social workers, and special educators, music therapists make an evaluation of how a client may be helped through a music program. They determine what goals and objectives can probably be met and plan musical activities and experiences which are likely to meet them, both on an individual and group basis. Therapists treat patients of all age groups, ranging from disturbed small children and adolescents to adults who suffer from mental illness of many types and varying degrees of seriousness. As members of the mental health team, music therapists devise programs to achieve aims prescribed by attending psychiatrists, and the treatment results are evaluated periodically.

The mentally retarded, cerebral palsied, crippled, and blind make up a group that is second only to the mentally ill in numbers receiving music therapy.

Music therapists may devise programs of many kinds in an effort to gain and to hold the patient's interest. Much depends upon the patient's potential for training, for what would be possible for one would be inappropriate for another. Group singing is commonly used.

Musical appreciation and musical education is appealing to others. Every effort is made to improve skills acquired in past years and to develop an interest which will, in itself, give a new dimension to normal living.

It should be noted, however, that unlike most music programs, music therapy programs focus on the well-being of the client rather than a perfected musical product. Voice as well as traditional and nontraditional instruments and music are utilized and individual lessons are provided. In addition, instrumental and/or vocal music is often combined with body movements as a part of therapy.

Music therapists may find employment in a variety of facilities in all parts of the country. They are usually employed in psychiatric hospitals, mental retardation centers, physical disability treatment and training institutions, day-care centers, nursing homes, special education programs, community mental-health centers, special services agencies, and other related facilities.

As in many therapy situations, music therapists work very closely with their clients and must be able to relate to them and their problems in a warm professional manner. The work is not always a relaxing, pleasurable experience. The process of strengthening discipline and changing behavior can temporarily arouse anxiety and negative attitudes. Music therapists must be able to deal with these problems when they arise and use tact and resourcefulness in solving them. They often must work in close cooperation with therapists in other disciplines when physical facilities are shared to plan and schedule activities. Standard work hours are usual, but music therapists may be called on from time to time to work evening hours and weekends.

Job Requirements

The amount and type of professional training and preparation required for employment as a music therapist often varies from employer to employer, and there are people working in the field who have advanced degrees and others who are not trained in academic institutions. However, as the field grows, standard educational requirements are being more rigidly established. The minimum training and preparation currently recommended by the two associations that certify and register music therapists includes a baccalaureate degree in music therapy plus completion of a 6-month internship in an approved facility. It is to the student's advantage to attend a school which combines clinical experience and classroom work at the same time. Courses leading to the bachelor's degree in music therapy include psychology, sociology, music ther-

apy, anthropology, music, and general education courses.

Licensure is not required of music therapists at the present time except for those working in public schools, who must be licensed as special educators in the State in which they are employed. Certification and registration may be obtained from the American Association for Music Therapists or the National Association of Music Therapists on completion of both the prescribed academic course of study at a recognized university and a 6-month clinical internship at an approved clinical-training facility. Certification and registration are not required for employment, but many employers include eligibility for them as part of their hiring policy.

Opportunities

Employment prospects depend very much on healthcare trends, economic conditions, and the role of government in health care, and projections are difficult to forecast. However, today, music therapy is being used in a wider variety of treatment institutions than ever before and has been gaining acceptance as an alternate form of traditional health care. If these two trends continue it should have a favorable influence on the demand for music therapists.

Many fields are an end in themselves, and those who enter them usually enter with the aim of making a career of performing the work they have chosen. Teaching is such a field and so is music therapy. Music therapists usually enter this career field because there is something stimulating about working with people in a therapy situation that involves music. There are rewards within the field itself and there is always the possibility of being recognized for outstanding accomplishments or for having developed new and innovative methods. Advancement is possible in this field but almost always requires the music therapist to devote less time to actual music therapy and more to administrative duties. For example, the usual path of advancement is from music therapist to department supervisor, coordinator of an activities therapy department, or other related administrative position. So, in addition to the advancement requirements of experience and/or additional education, the therapist must agree to accept an administrative position in order to be promoted. One other avenue of what might be considered advancement, but is often thought of as a separate career area, is university teaching. For a teaching position, the music therapist will need both clinical experience and a graduate degree.

For further information, contact:

American Association for Music Therapy
National Association for Music Therapy

VIII. Occupational Therapist
Occupational therapist, registered (OTR)

Occupational therapists are health professionals who provide services to all types of individuals whose lives have been impaired by physical, psychological, or developmental problems. They assist these individuals to achieve the highest level of functioning possible and to reduce or eliminate the need for continued healthcare services. Like most of the other health professionals, occupational therapists usually work as a member of a medical team, which may include a physician, physical therapist, vocational counselor, and other related professionals. The team members examine the patient in terms of their individual specialties and consult with each other to arrive at an overall evaluation of the patient's capacities, skills, and abilities. Occupational therapists study those aspects of the evaluation related to occupational therapy and discuss them with the patient. Together they develop short-and long-term goals and the means by which they may be achieved. It is a complex process, and many factors are taken into consideration as a course of therapy is developed.

Therapists select appropriate activities that are suited to the physical capacity, intelligence level, and interests of each patient. These activities are designed to develop independence, prepare patients for a return to work, restore basic functions, and aid in adjustment to disabilities. The course of therapy almost always involves goal-directed activities because these activities are the primary therapy tools. For instance, occupational therapists may help patients develop an interest in ceramics, jewelry making, woodworking, weaving, or other craft activities that will improve motor skills, strength, endurance, concentration, motivation, or other physical and/or mental capacities. Other patients might be enrolled in classes which will help them prepare for specific occupational goals or develop the functional skills, abilities, and capacities needed for the tasks of everyday living.

Beside the ability to teach and to communicate with handicapped people, and a solid background of knowledge of the physical sciences and medicine, occupational therapists need specific knowledge in the various working skills used in therapy. Among these skills are leatherwork, jewelry making, ceramics, woodwork, metalwork, textile crafts, and printing. They also need to know the skills of daily living and simple homemaking. In addition to planning, directing, and participating in therapeutic goal-directed activities, occupational therapists also make and apply splints; provide patients with guidance and instruction; assist in the selection and use of equipment to help patients adapt to the environment and/or impairment; recommend changes in home or work environments to promote the patient's safety and ease of function; and determine or develop other appropriate treatments and activities. Therapists may also organize educational activities, such as the study of language or creative writing, or may organize dramatic groups. For activities such as these, they generally call upon the assistance of a professional in the particular field. Though they cannot be expert in all these activities, occupational therapists must know enough about them to understand their therapeutic values and to set them into motion.

Often physical or mental disability is so severe that patients can no longer work in their former occupations or professions. In such cases, therapists may discover some other skill or talent which patients can develop and use, and this becomes the goal of the therapy. Occupational therapists regularly prepare reports for the information of members of the health team. A report may cover, for example, an account of the progress of a physically disabled patient who has been assigned tasks of increasing difficulty. Or it may cover the progress being made by crippled children in developing muscle coordination through play with therapeutic toys.

While there are no recognized areas of specialization in this career, occupational therapists do tend to work with certain types of disability and age groups. For instance, of the occupational therapists engaged in direct service, approximately 60 percent work principally with persons who have physical disabilities and 40 percent work with patients who have psychological or emotional problems. Twenty-five percent work exclusively with persons under the age of 20, and 10 percent work exclusively with the aged. Occupational therapists are employed in a variety of facilities. Hospitals-including short-and long-term general, psychiatric, and other specialties—appear to be the major single employer of occupational therapists, employing approximately 40 percent of the total employed, while rehabilitation centers and schools each employ about 15 percent. Skilled nursing or intermediate-care facilities hire just under 10 percent, and about 5 percent find work in community mental-health programs. The remainder are scattered among private practice, home-health agencies, educational settings, day-care centers, and similar institutions. Working conditions are generally considered good but do vary among facilities.

The actual range of conditions might be best described as running from adequate to excellent, but there are many factors of a highly personal nature that go into such a judgment. An individual who is interested in an occupational therapy career should visit some facilities that employ occupational therapists to form an individual opinion.

Job Requirements
Persons considering this career must be able to work with people of all kinds and all ages, with temperaments and personali-

ties that are likely to be as varied as patient illnesses and handicaps. To gain their confidence, it is necessary to have a warm, friendly personality that inspires both trust and respect. In addition to these qualities, it is also necessary to have ingenuity and imagination in adapting activities to individual needs. The potential therapist also needs to be skilled, patient, and resourceful in teaching, since patients often present unusual and difficult learning problems. This occupation offers an excellent opportunity to combine an interest in teaching with an interest in helping people in distress and extreme need.

The educational preparation for occupational therapy requires 4 years of college training leading to the degree of bachelor of science. All occupational therapy programs offered by colleges and universities are approved by the American Medical Association's Committee on Allied Health Education and Accreditation, in collaboration with American Occupational Therapy Association.

In addition to the 4 years of academic preparation, a clinical training period is required in order to qualify for professional registration. In most schools, this clinical experience takes from 6 to 9 months.

For those who already have a degree before enrolling in a program of occupational therapy, there is an advanced-standing course of from 18 to 22 months, divided between academic and clinical work. There are also master's degree programs offered in several universities.

Although supervised clinical experience is part of all the approved programs, compensation during this period varies widely. Some institutions offer no compensation at all, others provide maintenance, and still others give a cash stipend in lieu of maintenance. The college preparation for occupational therapy emphasizes physical and behavioral sciences such as anatomy, physiology, neurology, psychology, and sociology. Other subjects include manual and creative skills, educational subjects, and recreational activities.

In 1977, 56 U.S. colleges offered programs in occupational therapy leading to the required degree and accredited by the American Medical Association and the American Occupational Therapy Association.

Graduates of accredited schools of occupational therapy are eligible to take the national registration examination conducted by the American Occupational Therapy Association. On successful completion of the examination, therapists become professionally qualified to practice and are entitled to use the initials OTR after their name. In addition to this, they automatically become certified and are eligible to become members of the association.

Opportunities

Since 1970, the occupational therapy profession has experienced a growth rate averaging nearly 10 percent per year. While no one can predict the future with absolute certainty, it is anticipated that employment in this occupation will continue to grow. However, the number of occupational therapy graduates is increasing every year and new graduates are expected to balance the demand created by new openings and replacement needs caused by those who leave the field for one reason or another. Therefore, there may be considerable competition for available positions, particularly in the more desirable areas. Prospective occupational therapy students are advised to check with professional occupational therapy associations, schools, and facilities that employ occupational therapists to obtain information on current needs and trends.

The usual path of advancement in this work is from staff therapist, usually the occupational therapist's first job, to senior therapist, after gaining approximately 3 years experience, to supervisor/administrative therapist, after approximately 5 years experience. Advancement, of course, is not automatic but is based on the occupational therapist's professional growth, development, and often additional education. Also, changes in this progression are not uncommon and other types of related advancement positions are possible. For instance, sometimes occupational therapists work under independent contract either providing direct occupational therapy or consulting services. Another possibility is teaching, in which the steps leading toward advancement are completely different.

For further information, contact: American Occupational Therapy Association

IX. Occupational Therapy Assistant

Occupational therapy assistants work under the direction of professional occupational therapists in carrying out rehabilitation programs. They relieve the therapists of many routine tasks, allowing them to serve a greater number of patients. Therapists and assistants are partners in the rehabilitation of patients impaired by physical, psychological, or developmental problems.

Occupational therapy assistants help occupational therapists to plan and carry out educational, vocational, and recreational activities programs aimed at helping patients to regain the use of those capacities that remain after accident, disease, or deformity. They teach and assist patients to develop skills in self care and in work-related, creative, and recreational activities. Since they wopk very closely with patients, occupational therapy assistants observe them and make reports to the occupational therapist on the patients' progress and development. In addition, occupational therapy assistants perform many other tasks such as ordering, preparing, and laying out materials; helping to make splints, braces, and other assistive devices; and maintaining tools and equipment. While there are no recognized specialization areas in this career, occupational therapist assistants tend to be assigned to work with certain types of disability or age group populations. For instance, one therapist may work almost exclusively with physical disabilities, another with psychological or emotional problems, a third may work exclusively with patients under 20 years of age, and a fourth may work only with the aged.

Many types of facilities located throughout the country employ occupational therapy assistants. Hospitals are the largest employer, employing about 50 percent. The remainder are divided among nursing homes, schools for handicapped children and the mentally retarded, rehabilitation and day-care centers, clinics, and similar institutions. Working conditions are generally considered good, although they vary from facility to facility. However, since many personal factors go into making an evaluation of facilities and working conditions, the prospective occupational therapy assistant should visit several facilities that employ occupational therapy assistants to form an individual opinion.

Job Requirements

High school graduates can prepare for this career by completing a 2-year associate degree program in an ac-credited university or junior or community college. These programs include a minimum of 2 months of supervised practical experience. They also include courses covering structure and function of the human body, growth and development from childhood to old age, physical disability, and mental illness. In addition, there is training in therapeutic skills and crafts. Graduates of a program approved by the American Occupational Therapy Association are eligible for certification as an occupational therapy assistant (COTA) if they meet specified education and experience requirements. At present, there are no licensure requirements for occupational therapy assistants. Continuing education is not a requirement for occupational therapy assistants. However, additional course work not only keeps the assistant up to date on what is happening in the profession but helps to develop expertise, making the employee more valuable and more qualified for promotion.

Opportunities

The demand for occupational therapy assistants is expected to continue to grow at a steady rate. The number of training programs offered by schools is also expected to increase, but the supply of graduates is expected to fall short of the demand for qualified occupational therapist assistants. The best possibilities for advancement are in the larger facilities, where assistants may be given more and more responsibilities as they gain experience. After occupational therapy assistants have completed 4 years of acceptable experience, they are eligible and may apply to take the American Occupational Therapy Association examination to become occupational therapists.

For further information, contact: American Occupational Therapy Association

X. Orthotic-Prosthetic Technician

Orthotic-prosthetic technicians make, repair, and maintain orthotic and prosthetic devices, under the guidance of an orthotist/prosthetist. Orthotic devices include braces and surgical supports, while prosthetic devices refer to such items as artificial limbs or plastic cosmetic devices. Technicians, working under the supervision of a orthotist-prosthetist, follow prescription specifications to determine the type of device to be made and the tools and materials required. When working with orthotic devices, they bend, form, and fasten parts of metal braces to conform to measurements, using a variety of handtools. They shape plastic and metal around casts of the patients' body or limbs and cover and pad brace structures with such materials as rubber, plastic, leather, and felt.

When working on prosthetic devices, they lay out the work; mark the sizes of parts, using precision measuring instruments; and follow prescribed specifications. Using many kinds of tools and a variety of materials such as wood, plastic, metal, or fabric, they make parts to assemble into different types of prostheses.

Orthotic-prosthetic technicians are also responsible for repairing and maintaining orthoses and prostheses as directed by the orthotist/prosthetist. Although technicians do not take part in direct patient care activities, they have the important responsibility of insuring that the workmanship and quality of devices produced meet acceptable standards. Technicians can specialize in orthotics or in prosthetics, or, when qualified, can perform in both orthotics and prosthetics.

Job Requirements

The American Board for Certification in Orthotics and Prosthetics registers orthotic-prosthetic technicians who meet specific requirements. Candidates for registration must have at least a 10th grade education and have a minimum of 2 years of work experience in making orthoses and/or prostheses. This experience must have been obtained under the supervision of a Certified Orthotist (CO), Certified Prosthetist (CP) or a Certified Prosthetist-Orthotist (CPO). Candidates who have completed a formal educational program in orthotics or prosthetics given in an institution accredited by the board are not required to meet the experience requirements. In addition, candidates must qualify on an examination administered by the board.

Candidates who pass the technician examination in orthotics are awarded the designation of Registered Technician (Orthotics) RT (O). Candidates passing the. examination in prosthetics are designated as Registered Technician (Prosthetics) RT (P). Those who pass the combined examination for orthotic-prosthetic technician receive the designation of Registered Technician (Orthotics-Prosthetics) RT (OP).

Opportunities

Employment prospects for qualified orthotic-prosthetic technicians are generally favorable and are expected to remain so during the next several years. Advancement opportunities in this field are good and are based on work experience and completion of further education and training. By meeting prescribed training and education requirements, technicians can advance to the practitioner-level positions of Certified Orthotist, Certified Prosthetist, or Certified Prosthetist-Orthotist.

For further information, contact:
American Orthotic and Prosthetic Association

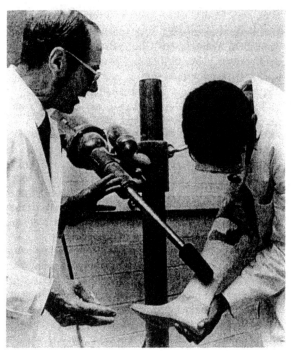

XI. Orthotist

Orthotists provide care to persons with limb or spine disabilities by fitting and making devices called orthoses. These devices are orthopedic braces which support weakened body parts or help to correct physical defects such as spinal deformities. Orthotists work with physicians, following physicians' prescriptions or helping to develop prescriptions for orthoses. They examine and judge patients' orthotic needs and make recommendations based on individual problems. Orthotists are responsible for designing each orthosis; selecting proper materials; and making all measurements, model changes and layouts of designs. In addition, they are responsible for making sure that the devices fit and work properly, for making necessary adjustments, and for teaching patients the use and care of these devices.

Orthotists maintain accurate patient records and keep up with developments in this field in order to provide patients with the best possible care. They supervise or-thotic/prosthetic technicians and other laboratory workers involved in making orthoses. They lecture and teach their specialty to colleagues or others who are interested in this field or work in research activities. Some orthotists are qualified to function as prosthetists and provide patients with artificial replacements for limbs or other body parts. In such cases they carry the professional designation of prosthetist-orthotist.

Orthotists are employed in privately owned facilities or laboratories; rehabilitation centers; hospitals; and Federal, State, and local rehabilitation agencies.

Job Requirements

Persons considering this career area must have skillful hands, be able to work with various types of tools, and possess mechanical ability. In addition, candidates must show patience and have a responsible attitude toward their work and a concern for detail and accuracy. Candidates must also be concerned for the welfare of the disabled and be able to communicate with both patients and members of the rehabilitation team. High school courses considered useful in preparing for this career include physics, chemistry, mathematics, biology, and shop courses in metal, wood, and plastics.

The American Board for Certification in Orthotics and Prosthetics is the certifying agency for professional practitioners in this field. They set education and training standards for othotists and administer an examination to all candidates applying for certification status. The usual method of preparing for practitioner certification is to obtain a bachelor's degree in orthotics from an accredited college or university, combined with 1 year of clinical experience. However, persons who hold an associate degree in orthotics or another area can also qualify by completing three special courses in orthotics at an accredited training facility and obtaining 2 years of clinical experience. Persons with a bachelor's degree in a different area of specialization may also qualify for practitioner certification by completing postgraduate training in orthotics, ranging in length from 4 to 8 months, combined with 1 or 2 years of acceptable work experience. Beginning in 1980 the minimum educational requirement will be a bachelor's degree.

Candidates who pass the certification examination are awarded the designation of

Certified Orthotist (CO). Those orthotists who are also qualified to practice as prosthetists, and who pass the examination in both specialties, are given the designation of Certified Prosthetist-Orthotist (CPO).

Opportunities

Employment opportunities for qualified orthotists are generally good and are expected to remain so during the next several years. Advancement in this field takes different forms, depending on the employment location, but is generally based on work experience and skill level. Orthotists can advance to supervisory and administrative positions, and in some cases may become self-employed as private practitioners.

For further information, contact:
American Orthotic and Prosthetic Association

XII. Physical Therapist
Physiotherapist

Physical therapists are health-care practitioners who plan and adminster physical treatment for patients referred by a physician in order to restore bodily functions, relieve pain, and prevent disability following disease, injury, or loss of a body part. Physical therapy has value in the treatment of a wide variety of diseases and injuries, such as multiple sclerosis, nerve injuries, chest conditions, amputations, fractures, arthritis, and cerebral palsy. Initially, physical therapists review and evaluate the patient's condition and medical records, perform indicated tests or measurements, and evaluate the findings. They use the findings to establish a patient care plan which includes setting short- and long-term goals and appropriate treatment procedures for the patient. The goal of physical therapists is to help patients to reach maximum performance levels and to regain a place in society while adjusting to the limiting effects of disabilities. When meeting a patient for the first time, physical therapists, like physicians, keep in mind the importance of preparing the patient emotionally for what is to come. They must be sensitive to the problems of the patient, who is made vulnerable by disability or disease.

Since treatments may be prolonged and often require active participation, the full cooperation of patients is very important. As a first step, therefore, physical therapists familiarize themselves with the patients' personal backgrounds, as well as their medical histories, and make an effort to gain their confidence and cooperation. The therapist-patient relationship often determines success or failure in involving patients in their own treatment. This is especially true of children. When working with children, therapists must do their best to help the parents as well as children to understand the treatment.

As members of the health team, therapists help patients overcome their disabilities through the use of exercise, heat, cold, electricity, ultasound, and massage. To carry out these tasks, therapists must have detailed knowledge of human anatomy and physiology and know what steps may be taken to correct disease and injury.

For example, in the case of children with a birth defect, physicians call upon physical therapists who may perform a muscle evaluation in order to determine the extent of the damage. On the basis of the muscle test, plans are made for the kind of physical therapy the children need. Physical therapists then carry out the plan of treatment.

In working with such children, physical therapists give the exercises that restore weakened muscles to normalcy. Treatment may include water exercises in warm baths or pools, hot packs, electricity (currents that stimulate paralyzed muscles), ultraviolet rays, and massage. When children must be fitted with braces or crutches, therapists teach walking with the aid of these appliances.

Treatment can be more effective and progress faster if patients and their families understand the purpose and plan and know just how they can help. Physical therapy services include instructing patients and their families in how to carry on prescribed treatment programs at home. They may need specific instruction in the techniques of muscle reduction or in the care and use of braces or prosthetic appliances. Physical therapists may personally conduct the treatment program or supervise a program conducted by a physical therapist assistant.

Physical therapists work in hospitals, rehabilitation centers, nursing homes, home-health agencies, public health agencies, school districts, private practices, and the armed forces. Therapists usually work closely with other people including the patient, patient's family, and other health-care practitioners. Physical therapists are generally required to be physically fit, since the practice of physical therapy requires the worker to lift, climb, stoop, stand, and kneel. Additionally, therapists should have manual dexterity, good visual acuity and hearing, and be able to communicate both orally and in writing.

Job Requirements

Adaptability, emotional stability, tact, and an outgoing personality are necessary in this profession. Physical therapy also takes a great deal of patience and the ability to work toward a long-range goal, even though the progress may sometimes seem slow. There are three education plans which prepare students for professional qualification in physical therapy. The first is a 4-year program leading to a bachelor's degree in physical therapy. The second is a 12- to 16-month certificate program for students who hold a bachelor's degree in a subject other than physical therapy. And last is a 2-year graduate program which leads to a master's degree for students with a bachelor's degree and the, necessary background. Each of these plans includes a minimum of 4 months of clinical education and experience in health-care facilities where students care for patients under the supervision of a qualified physical therapist. The basic curriculum of an accredited program in physical therapy is generally divided into several areas: a liberal arts program which emphasizes the humani-

ties and social studies; study of biological sciences including anatomy, physiology, and pathology; and a major emphasis in physical sciences like chemistry and physics, including the fundamental principles of mechanics, thermodynamics, light, sound, and electricity. Specialization courses provide the fundamental knowledge and skills required to treat patients, and supervised clinical practice is necessary to complete the course. Both the American Medical Association's Committee on Allied Health Education and Accreditation and the American Physical Therapy Association independently accredit educational programs in physical therapy.

All States, the District of Columbia, Virgin Islands, and Puerto Rico require licensure to practice physical therapy in the U.S. Each State, the District of Columbia, Virgin Islands and Puerto Rico have their own licensing requirements, and physical therapists must comply with the legal requirements of the area in which they practice.

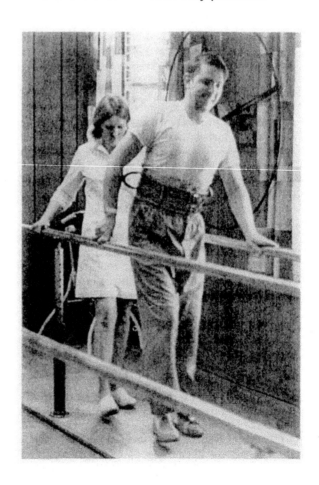

Opportunities

Employment prospects for qualified physical therapists are expected to be favorable through the next decade. Many openings go unfilled each year because of the lack of physical therapists and the maldistribution of those who are available. In the near future, the greatest demand for physical therapists is expected in primary health care and preventive services, as well as in the traditional areas of rehabilitation.

Physical therapists can advance in several different ways. They may advance from staff physical therapist positions in hospital physical therapy departments to department director, and, if the service is large enough, they may advance to coordinator or director of rehabilitation services. Therapists who have a master's degree can advance to supervisory, administrative, or teaching positions.

For further information, contact: American Physical Therapy Association

XIII. Physical Therapist Assistant
Physical therapy assistant
Physical therapy technician

Physical therapist assistants are skilled health practitioners who administer physical therapy to patients in treatment programs, under the direction of qualified physical therapists. They generally work with patients who have relatively stable conditions and use a variety of treatment techniques. They administer exercises; massage; heat, light, sound, water, electrical and infrared treatments; and use hot or cold packs to treat patients. Assistants instruct and assist patients to learn or improve their ability to walk, climb, and move from one location to another and to acquire skills needed for daily living. They observe patients during treatment to gather information on their responses and progress and report findings to the physical therapist, either orally or in writing. They also instruct patients in the use and care of artificial limbs, braces, and other devices such as crutches, canes, walkers, and wheelchairs.

Physical therapist assistants are employed in hospitals, rehabilitation centers, nursing homes, home-health agencies, public-health agencies, schools, private practices, and the armed forces.

Assistants work closely with patients, the patients' families, and other health-care personnel. They must be physically and mentally fit and be able to lift, climb, stoop, stand, and kneel. Additional requirements for physical therapist assistants are good hearing and visual acuity and the ability to communicate both orally and in writing.

Job Requirements

Preparation for this career area includes completion of high school and graduation from a 2-year accredited program leading to an associate degree in physical therapy. These programs are offered in junior and community colleges and combine academic studies with supervised clinical experience.

There are licensing requirements for physical therapist assistants in 23 States. The licensure boards in these States administer an examination to applicants who meet the qualifications set forth in the State Physical Therapy Practice Act. At present, there are no certification requirements for physical therapist assistants. For information about licensing requirements, candidates should contact the appropriate State licensing agency.

Opportunities

The employment prospects for physical therapist assistant are good through the next several years. This outlook is based on the trend toward expanding physical therapy programs in many different types of facilities and on increased public awareness of the need for professional rehabilitation services.

Advancement in this work is based on work experience, which leads to greater responsibilities, and on advanced education. Assistants who engage in continued education can become fully qualified therapists by completing an accredited program of study.

For further information, contact: American Physical Therapy Association

XIV. Prosthetist

Prosthetists provide care to persons with partial or total loss of a limb by fitting and making artificial limbs known as prostheses. They consult with a physician, follow physician prescriptions, or help in developing prescriptions for the prostheses. Prosthetists talk with and examine patients and make recommendations for meeting their individual needs. After taking careful and accurate measurements and making any needed casts, they design the prosthesis, select the necessary materials, and prepare a layout of the design. Before completing the final model, they give the patient a fitting and make any necessary adjustments to insure that the device gives the patient comfort and function. Prosthetists instruct patients in the use and care of devices, maintain complete records of patient activity, and provide patients with the best possible care by keeping current on new technology in this field. Prosthetists supervise orthotic/prosthetic technicians and other laboratory workers engaged in making prostheses. Prosthetists engage in teaching activities or perform research work in this field. Some prosthetists are qualified, by additional training, to function as or-thotists. In such cases they carry the professional designation of prosthetist-orthotist.

Job Requirements

Persons considering this career area must have manual dexterity, be able to work with various types of tools, and possess mechanical ability. In addition, candidates must display patience, have a responsible attitude toward their work, and have a concern for detail and accuracy. Candidates must also have a sense of concern for the welfare of the disabled and be able to communicate effectively with both patients and members of the rehabilitation team. High school courses considered useful in preparing for this career include physics, chemistry, mathematics, biology, and shop courses in metal, wood, and plastics.

The American Board for Certification in Orthotics and Prosthetics is the certifying agency for professional practitioners in this field. They set education and training standards for prosthetists and administer an examination to all candidates applying for certification. The usual method of preparing for practitioner certification is to obtain a bachelor's degree in prosthetics from an accredited college or university, combined with 1 year of clinical experience. However, persons who hold an associate degree in prosthetics or another area can also qualify by completing three specified courses in prosthetics at an accredited training facility and obtaining 2 years of clinical experience. Persons with a bachelor's degree in a different area of specialization may also qualify for practitioner certification by completing post-graduate training in prosthetics, ranging in length from 4 to 8 months, combined with 1 or 2 years of acceptable work experience. Beginning in 1980, the minimum educational requirement will be a bachelor's degree.

Candidates who pass the certification examination are awarded the designation of Certified Prosthetist (CP). Those prosthetists who are also qualified to practice as orthotists, and who pass the examination in both specialties, are given the designation of

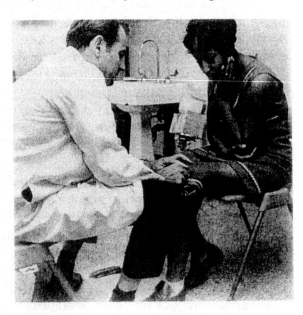

Certified Prosthetist-Orthotist (CPO).

Opportunities

Employment prospects for qualified prosthetists are generally favorable and this trend is expected to continue during the next several years. Advancement in this field takes different forms, depending on the place of employment, but is generally based on work experience and level of skill. Qualified prosthetists often move into supervisory jobs, and in some cases may become self-employed as private practitioners.

For further information, contact:
American Orthotic and Prosthetic Association

XV. Recreation Therapist
Activities therapist
Recreation specialist
Therapeutic recreation specialist

Recreation therapy is a specialized field in which recreation services are used to help individuals to recover from or adjust to illness, disability, or a specific social problem. Recreation therapists organize, develop, and carry out therapeutic recreational activities which help to meet this goal. These recreational programs are carried out in health facilities or community settings and include such activities as athletics, dancing, arts and crafts, music, movies, parties, gardening, and camping. Each of these is used to provide patients with the benefits of exercise, social participation, and group interaction. The therapeutic recreation activities that they conduct are designed to assist patients to develop interpersonal relationships, resocialize, relieve anxiety and tension, and develop confidence needed to participate in social activities.

Recreation therapists are an important part of the health team; they observe the physical, mental, and social progress of patients and contribute information and progress reports for use in meeting treatment goals. Recreation therapists assist patients in readjusting recreational needs to the activities offered by the community in which they live, based on knowledge of community resources and programs. Therapists also train groups of volunteers and students in techniques of recreation therapy. In addi-

tion, therapists work with various educational institutions to develop courses in the field of therapeutic recreation.

Recreation therapists are employed in a variety of public and private facilities including State or private hospitals for the mentally ill or mentally retarded; prisons, and juvenile retention homes; orphanages; veterans' hospitals for both general and psychiatric patients; armed forces hospitals; homes for the aged; schools for the blind and rehabilitation centers for the physically handicapped. Others work in day-care centers; clinics; private and public schools; recreation centers; camps; and private community agencies. No general statement can be made about working conditions since they vary widely from facility to facility. Physical handicaps are not barriers to employment in this work as long as the individual has adjusted suitably to the disability.

Job Requirements

The educational minimum for entry as a professional in this field is a bachelor's degree in recreation, with emphasis on rehabilitation or therapeutic recreation, from an accredited college or university. In addition, students must complete 400 hours of clinical training in a university or college-affiliated hospital.

In some cases, an associate degree or certificate in therapeutic recreation is acceptable for entry into lower level jobs in this field, which involve limited responsibilities.

The American Association for Rehabilitation Therapy (AART) is the registration body for recreation therapists, and although registration is not a condition of employment, many therapists choose to do so. The requirements for registration as a recreation therapist include membership in AART, 2 years experience, as a recreation therapist in a health-care facility, letters of recommendation, and copies of college transcripts.

Opportunities

Employment prospects for recreation therapists are favorable. The job market is expected to expand steadily in line with the expansion of health facilities throughout the country, as well as increases in population, particularly among the aging.

Advancement possibilities for recreation therapists vary widely among facilities, but, in general, promotions are based on experience, skill level, and education. In local, State, and Federal facilities, advancement can be achieved through the traditional methods of competitive civil service. Therapists in lower level positions who have an associate degree or certificate can advance to professional status in the field by completing the required bachelor's program in recreation. Therapists who obtain a master's degree can qualify for positions in administration, research, and teaching.

For further information, contact:
American Association for Rehabilitation Therapy National Therapeutic Recreation Society

XVI. Speech Pathologist and Audiologist
Speech correctionist
Speech and language pathologist/ audiologist
Speech therapist

Speech pathologists and audiologists provide specialized help to people with problems of speaking and hearing. Speech-language pathologists are primarily concerned with persons who have speech, language, and voice disorders, while audiologists concentrate on individuals with hearing problems.

The goal of speech pathologists and audiologists is to help children and adults overcome such problems as lisping, cleft palate, impaired hearing and talking difficulties resulting from cerebral palsy, emotional or physical disturbance or retardation, stuttering, or foreign dialect.

Speech pathologists diagnose and evaluate the individuals' speech and language abilities. They plan, direct, and conduct treatment programs to restore or develop patients' communication skills, regardless of the cause of the disorder. Speech pathologists can and do work closely with a number of other professionals, including audiologists, physicians, psycholo-

gists, social workers, counselors, physical and occupational therapists, and educators.

Audiologists are concerned with the prevention of hearing impairment and the conservation of hearing in children and adults. Audiologists assess the type and degree of hearing impairment. They then add their findings to educational, medical, social, behavioral, and other diagnostic data. After evaluating all of the available information, they may plan, direct, conduct or participate in aural rehabilitation programs which meet the needs of the individual patient. These programs include such activities as hearing-aid selection and orientation, auditory training, speech reading, speech conservation, counseling, and guidance. Audiologists, like speech pathologists, often work closely with other professionals and as consultants to educational, medical, and other professional groups.

Speech pathologists and audiologists work in public and private schools; colleges and universities; clinics; research centers; hospitals; speech and hearing centers; private industry; private practice; and Federal State, and local agencies.

Job Requirements

People who seek careers working directly with handicapped children and adults must have a real concern for people with physical and psychological problems and a sincere desire to help them. Equally important is the ability to work with such problems objectively. The potential speech pathologist or audiologist should have a warm, friendly personality that inspires confidence in the person being helped. Patience and perseverance are also needed, since rehabilitation may be a slow process. Relating well to children is a definite asset, since much of the work in speech rehabilitation is done with youngsters.

To qualify as a speech pathologist or audiologist, a person must have a master's degree in speech pathology or audiology. As part of the requirements for the master's degree, an individual will have numerous supervised clinical experiences. The student may also complete sufficient courses to be certified by the American Speech and Hearing Association (ASHA) and/or licensed by his or her State. A number of preprofessional degree programs in speech pathology or audiology are available.

Although programs leading to a master's degree in speech pathology or audiology vary from college to college, course work will include normal development and function of speech, language, and hearing; anatomy and physiology; the nature of disorders of speech, language, and hearing; the evaluation of speech, language, and hearing; clinical methods; and research.

Speech pathologists and audiologists may hold a variety of credentials, including State license, teaching credentials, and the American Speech and Hearing Association's Certificate of Clinical Competence in either or both areas. The ASHA certificates require academic training at the master's level, 1 year of experience in the field, and the passing of a national examination. Since credential and licensure requirements may vary from State to State, the appropriate State agency should be contacted to determine what requirements must be met.

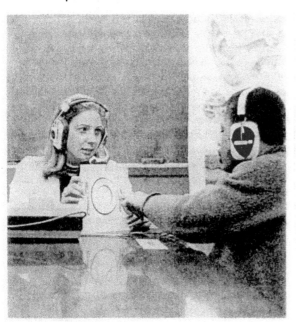

Opportunities

Employment prospects are expected to increase during the next decade. However, the competition for openings, especially in large urban areas, is expected to be keen.

Speech pathologists and audiologists may advance to administrative or supervisory positions such as clinic director or coordinator of clinical services. They may also become professors or department heads in colleges or universities, or choose to engage in research activities. Professional mobility is generally based on experience, skills, and level of education.

For further information, contact: American Speech and Hearing Association National Association for Hearing and Speech Action

XVII. Vocational Rehabilitation Counselor Rehabilitation counselor

Many different services go into rehabilitationthe process by which a sick or disabled person is restored to normal or near-normal functioning. One form of rehabilitation is concerned with repairing the damage done by illness or injury, and this is the responsibility of the physician. Another form of rehabilitation is concerned with restoring the person to a prior level of vocational performance or, if this is no longer possible, with preparing the individual for a new vocation. This is the function of vocational rehabilitation counseling. Most illnesses leave the patient with little or no residual handicap, while others may cause long-lasting or permanent damage to physical or mental functioning. Handicaps such as these may not only prevent the individual from taking up a former occupation, but may also demoralize the person to a point where the motivation to learn another trade or profession, or the courage to find another job, is no longer present.

Vocational rehabilitation counselors help handicapped or disabled persons to overcome these obstacles. Counselors help these persons decide on a realistic vocational goal and then help them work toward this goal-placement in a satisfactory job. This may involve not only extensive vocational training but also the reshaping of negative attitudes and the development of confidence and motivation. As soon as the injury or illness is brought under control and the patient is able to function again, vocational rehabilitation counselors help the individuals minimize any handicaps by capitalizing on other resources-aptitudes, skills, and interests. For example, counselors cannot create a new pair of eyes for a blinded watchmaker, but they can help by exploring other opportunities where manual deftness can be put to use, as in the production of electrical equipment. Through retraining, disabled Workers learn to apply their abilities to new jobs, sometimes closely related, sometimes far removed from their previous work. Even in the case of handicapped or retarded young people who have never worked at all and who may have been considered unemployable, counselors can frequently devise a training program that can lead to employment.

To learn as much as possible about the handicapped person, counselors conduct interviews with the individual, the family doctor, former teachers, former employers, and others. Counselors may administer various aptitude tests and psychological tests or refer individuals to a testing specialist. If emotional problems seem to be interfering with adjustment, psychologists or psychiatrists may be consulted. When enough has been learned about the individual, the next step is to develop a vocational plan. Both individuals and counselors share in the planning, and others who may be involved are also called in-family members, prospective employers or social workers.

The actual training generally takes place in a sheltered job situation, where the trainee may learn a new occupation without the competitive pressures of regular employment. While training is in process, counselors keep in touch with trainees to observe progress and to be of continued help. When the training is completed, counselors help trainees to find jobs. Counselors make followup visits to insure that individuals are adjusting adequately to the new work situation. To be of greatest help, counselors must know the employment situation and employment opportunities, especially those for handicapped people. In cases where handi-

capped individuals are unable to enter or re-enter the labor market, counselors work with them to effect the best possible adjustment within family and social situations. In many cases, rehabilitation counselors specialize in services for particular groups-the blind, paraplegics, the mentally ill, and the retarded. In addition, counselors divide their time between counseling and community activities in the interest of the overall program-for example, calling on employers to solicit jobs, keeping in touch with educators and other interested professional groups, and taking part in meetings of local organizations and other activities which will help to focus public attention on problems of the handicapped and the benefits of rehabilitation.

Many vocational rehabilitation counselors work in State and local rehabilitation agencies which are financed by Federal and State funds. They also are employed by Veterans Administration facilities, rehabilitation centers, sheltered workshops, hospitals, labor unions, insurance companies, special schools, and public and private job-placement agencies. Counselors usually observe a typical 40-hour week, although they sometimes participate in various after-hours community activities related to rehabilitation, because of the importance of out-of-office contacts and community relations to vocational rehabilitation. In the course of the day's work, counselors are in touch with many people in many places-with the handicapped and their families, physicians and other members of the hospital staff, professional people in welfare agencies and similar organizations, school people, local public employment offices, employers' groups and individual employers, labor unions, and other sources of jobs or job information.

Job Requirements
The minimum requirement for a beginner's job in rehabilitation counseling is a bachelor's degree, preferably in psychology or education. However, employers are placing increasing emphasis on a master's degree in this area. Some experience in

such related fields as vocational guidance and placement, personnel work, psychology, social work, or teaching also may be helpful. Master's programs require from 1 1/2 to 2 years of study and include courses in rehabilitation problems, counseling techniques, vocational guidance, occupational and medical information, test administration and evaluation, psychology, statistics, and personnel administration. Additional courses may involve the community relations aspect of the rehabilitation program—for instance, public speaking, public relations, and methods of developing local job resources for the disabled. Some rehabilitation counselors take additional graduate work and earn a doctor's degree. This usually takes a total of from 4 to 6 years after college-part of it covered by the time required for the master's degree. Doctoral training usually goes into the more complex aspects of rehabilitation. This is supplemented by advanced work in the social sciences, and (as in other Ph.D programs) the student is expected to complete a considerable amount of original research.

There are currently no licensing requirements for vocational rehabilitation counselors, although licensing bills are beginning to be introduced in some States. However, some State agencies and private employers require some form of testing prior to offering employment, and increasingly they prefer individuals who are Certified Rehabilitation Counselors (CRC's). An individual is certified by the Commission on Rehabilitation Counselor Certification on the basis of an accepted level of competency, which includes both educational requirements and work experience. After receiving the initial certification, Certified Rehabilitation Couselors participate in a certification maintenance program to insure their continued proficiency in the field.

Opportunities

The present supply of rehabilitation counselors is inadequate to meet the needs of expanding groups of handicapped persons, and opportunities for qualified rehabilitation counselors are expected to remain good throughout the next decade. Counselors with graduate degrees in rehabilitation or a related field have the best opportunity for employment. Rehabilitation counselors can advance to supervisory or administrative positions after gaining sufficient experience and completing advanced training.

For further information, contact:
National Rehabilitation Counseling Association

GLOSSARY OF OCCUPATIONAL TERMS

TABLE OF CONTENTS

———————

GLOSSARY OF OCCUPATIONAL TERMS

ABSORPTION TOWER: Tank used to form acidic bisulfate, active agent in digesting wood, from ingredients such as sulfur dioxide, lime, manganese, and ammonia.

ABTURATOR CUP: *See* GAS CHECK.

ABUTMENT TOOTH: Tooth used for support or anchorage of partial dentures.

AGATE BEARING: A bearing made of agate used in small scales or precision balances where resistance to corrosion is essential.

AGE: A process of steaming printed or dyed cloth to develop and fix color.

AIR BAG: A heavy rubber tube used to expand inner tubes during manufacture and curing.

AIRGAP: The gap between the rotor and stator of an electric machine.

AIR LANCE: A long metal rod that carries compressed air to its tip. It is used for cleaning purposes.

AIRVEYOR: System by which small articles are blown by compressed air through pipes or ducts from one work station to another.

ALODIZE: A process for bathing metal in hot alodine solution to give it protective coating and surface for painting.

ALPHABETIC-NUMERIC: The characters which include letters of the alphabet, numerals, and other symbols, such as punctuation or mathematical symbols.

ALPHANUMERIC: A contraction of ALPHABETIC-NUMERIC.

ALVEOLOPLASTY: Use of plastic in bony socket of tooth (alveolus).

ANAEROBIC DEVICES: Instruments to remove oxygen from closed container or environment.

ANALOG COMPUTER: A COMPUTER which represents variables by physical analogies, thus any COMPUTER which solves problems by translating physical conditions, such as flow, temperature, pressure, angular position, or voltage, into related mechanical or electrical quantities and uses mechanical or electrical equivalent circuits as an analog for the physical phenomenon being investigated. In general it is a COMPUTER which uses an analog for each variable and produces analogs as OUTPUT. Thus an ANALOG COMPUTER measures continuously whereas a DIGITAL COMPUTER counts discretely.

ANISEIKONIA: Condition in which visual images appear different in size and form, causing eyestrain.

ARM BED: A tube mounted horizontally above sewing machine table. Used to sew articles of concave or tubular shape. Also known as cylinder bed.

ARTICULATOR: A hinged metal device on which plaster models of teeth and gums are mounted to simulate patient's mouth.

ASPIRATED: Dehydrated cells.

AUDIOLOGY: The study of hearing and of hearing disorders.

AUTOMATIC DATA PROCESSING (ADP): DATA PROCESSING performed by a system of electronic or electrical machines so interconnected and interacting as to reduce to a minimum the need for human assistance or intervention.

AUTOMATIC DATA-PROCESSING EQUIPMENT: A machine or group of interconnected machines, consisting of INPUT, STORAGE, computing, control, and OUTPUT devices, which use electronic circuitry in the main computing element to perform arithmetic and/or logical operations automatically by means of internally stored or externally controlled programed INSTRUCTIONS.

AUTOMATIC DATA-PROCESSING SYSTEM: The term descriptive of an intersecting assembly of procedures, processes, methods, personnel, and AUTOMATIC DATA-PROCESSING EQUIPMENT to perform a complex series of DATA PROCESSING operations.

BACK GREY CLOTH: Untreated fabric which is fed into fabric-printing machine between cloth to be printed and cylinder blanket to keep edges of latter and back of cloth clean.

BACK-ROLL LATHE: A veneer lathe equipped with knives mounted on impression roller that rotates counter to rotation of log. The knives score log lengthwise causing veneer to be peeled from log in narrow stave and hoop widths.

BAKER'S CHEESE: A cottage cheese whose curd has not been cooked or cut, used to make cheese tortes or cakes.

BALANCE PISTON: A disk placed on shaft of pump or compressor. Pressure is applied to one side to balance end thrust.

BALL MILL: A large steel vessel within which steel balls are rapidly tumbled. Material admitted to mill is crushed by balls and discharged through sifting screens at bottom.

BALL WARP: An untwisted rope of yarn wound on core, usually for dyeing or mercerizing.

BANBURY MIXER: A mixing machine, employing rotating paddles, which permits control over temperature of mixing batch through introduction of steam or coolants into coils within mixing chamber, or through electrical heating units. Commonly used in processing rubber or plastics compounds where chemical or physical changes are accomplished concurrently with mixing process.

BAND: Two plies of rubberized fabric pressed together with ends joined to form endless strip used in building pneumatic tires.

BAT: (I) A fluffy layer which is composed of interlaced and matted strands of fibrous material used for filling or insulating articles such as mattresses or comforters.

—— (II) A wooden spindle upon which felt stock, produced by GARNETT MACHINE, is wound.

—— (III) Plate of steel or pressed grit on which pressed grinding wheel is placed for drying and burning in kilns.

BATTER CLAW: A plaster form covered with felt cloth, attached to mechanical or hydraulic arm, used to spread clay on mold prior to jiggering operation.

BEAD: The core of rubber-impregnated strands of steel wire that form base of pneumatic tire and engage rim of wheel to which it is applied.

BEAM: (I) A cylinder upon which yarn or fabric is wound for dyeing or other processing.

—— (II) A rounded board upon which hides are stretched to be cleaned of hair and flesh prior to tanning operations.

BEAMING KNIFE: A two-handled concave knife blade, ground to fit curve of BEAM II, that is used to scrape hair and bits of flesh from hides or skins.

BEATING MACHINE: A machine equipped with leather strips which, when revolving, beat loose hair, dust, and foreign matter from fur pelts.

BEATING-UP MOTION: The third motion involved in weaving yarn into cloth.

BED CLAMP: *See* CLAMP MACHINE.

BELL REAMER: An expanding bit used to enlarge bottom of holes drilled to accommodate concrete pier footings. The conical shape of resulting hole anchors footing and serves as base for pier construction.

BENCH GRINDER: A small grinding machine for shaping and sharpening cutting edges of tools. It consists of motor, mounted on bench or floor stand, carrying grinding wheel at one or both ends of shaft.

BILGE: The greatest circumference of a barrel.

BILGE OF STAVE: The difference in width between ends and middle of a barrel stave.

BINDER: Tobacco leaves used to hold the inner parts of cigars in place before they are wrapped.

BISCUIT PEG: A handtool used to spread and press the powdered clay into cracks.

BIT: That portion of a smoking pipe held in the mouth and which forms part of the stem. Both stem and bit are often termed bit.

BITE BLOCK: A wax reproduction of a denture used to study relationship of jaws and arrangement of teeth.

BITTER: A handtool used to cut tile to irregular contours.

BLANKET: A band of thick rubber running beneath cloth in cloth-printing machine. Its principal function is to support cloth being printed and to absorb excess dyestuff.

BLIND STITCH: A sewing stitch that does not completely penetrate the material in which it is made. Used to fasten lining into garments so that the stitches do not show on the outside.

BLOCK: A round piece of bronze with concave top used to facilitate the grinding of lenses on fine-grinding and polishing machines.

BLOCK DIAGRAM: (I) A graphical representation of the hardware in a COMPUTER system. The primary purpose of a BLOCK DIAGRAM is to indicate the paths along which information and/or control flows between the various parts of a COMPUTER system. It should not be confused with the term FLOW CHART.

—— (II) A coarser and less symbolic representation than FLOW CHART.

BLOCKER: One of a number of leather strips joined together for use as trimming for shoes.

BLOCKING MACHINE: An electric stove equipped with a grill on which BLOCKS, pitch, and lenses are heated. On depressing a lever, hot pitch is forced onto block surface.

BOARD: A sheet of varnished canvas, or a lightweight wooden board, upon which rubber slabs or parts are placed for transportation or storage.

BOARDING: (I) The process of softening leather and developing the grain by rubbing the surfaces together.

—— (II) The operation of shaping and drying hosiery on heated, metal, leg-shaped forms known as hosiery boarding forms or boards.

BOLSTER: The center beam of railroad car truck assembly.

BOLT: A block or section of a log.

BOOK: (I) Pieces of uncured gum rubber or rubber-coated fabric placed between cloth pages or canvas sheets to prevent cohesion.

—— (II) A bundle of half-leaves of tobacco from which stems have been removed. These are separated into right- and left-hand books since cigarmaking machinery works tobacco from only one side of the leaf.

BOX BLANK: The sides, ends, and bottom of a wire-bound box in process of manufacture.

BOX TOE: The toe of a shoe that has been reinforced to maintain its shape and to give reasonable protection to the wearer. Steel, plastic, leatherboard, leather, or glue or shellac stiffened canvas are used as reinforcing materials. Reinforcing process is known as boxing.

BRAIL: A long-handled dip net operated by ropes and pulleys, used for dipping fish from nets and traps.

BREAKER: A strip of loosely woven rubberized fabric applied to pneumatic tire before the tread is put on that distributes pressure when the tire is in contact with ground.

BROKE: Paper discarded because of dirt spots, wrinkles, tears, holes, or other defects, and paper trimmed from rolls or sheets by cutting machines. Wet broke is taken off wet press of paper machine. Broke is usually returned to beater for reprocessing into paper.

BULKING CELL: A rectangular enclosure with an open top and hinged door used to compress tobacco into a bulk.

BUNCH: Crushed or shredded filler leaves pressed together to form inner part of cigars, usually held in place by binder tobacco leaves which are rolled around them.

BUNG: The vent of a barrel or cask.

BUS BAR: Metal conductor forming a common junction between two or more electrical circuits.

BUSHING: Heat resistant metal device with 200-400

holes through which molten glass is extruded to manufacture fiber glass sliver.

BUTTON: A steel cylinder used on knitting machine to keep links of pattern chain from engaging and turning gears that activate shafts of machine.

CAKE: Synthetic thread piled into ring shape.

CALENDERING: An operation in the process of making rubber sheeting in which material is rolled to uniform thickness between rolls of CALENDER MACHINE.

CALENDER MACHINE: A machine designed to finish cloth, paper, or rubberized fabric by applying pressure to heavy rollers, some of which are heated. Two to ten rollers are used and various combinations of pressure, heat, and speed produce a variety of finishes.

CALENDER ROLLS: A set of rolls between which fabric receives final pressing during course of manufacture. Usually rolls are heated by steam.

CALIPER CHISEL: A chisel attached to one leg of caliper used to turn wood to specified diameter on wood lathe.

CALKING GUN: A metal cylinder equipped with nozzle, plunger, and lever used to apply calking compound.

CANT: A log that has been slabbed on one or more sides.

CAP-LEAD ASSEMBLIES: Metal cap with extending lead wire. Cap-lead assemblies are used in production of electronic units, such as resistors.

CAPSTAN: Drum-shaped device located between twisting-head and takeup spool of stranding machine.

CARD: A unit of pattern chain used on JACQUARD LOOM. It is a cardboard strip with holes similar to those in player-piano roll punched in it.

CARD CLOTHING FILLET: A long, narrow strip of card clothing consisting of thick foundation material in which are set many fine, closely spaced, wire teeth.

CARDING MACHINE: A machine consisting of cylinders of various sizes covered with wire teeth, used to prepare cotton, wool, and other fibers for spinning by removing impurities and arranging fibers approximately parallel. The carding machine receives fiber as raw stock or LAP II and delivers carded fiber as roving.

CARROTING: The brushing of furs with solution of mercury and nitric acid. This treatment opens sheaths surrounding each fur fiber and permits matting (felting) of fibers in subsequent operations.

CASE CLAMP: See CLAMP MACHINE.

CASING FLUID: A flavoring solution applied to tobacco to give it distinctive taste. Usually made according to carefully guarded plant formulas from ingredients, such as tonka beans, rum, licorice, and sugar.

CAUL: A sheet of wood, metal, or other material placed between layers of glued material in press to distribute pressure uniformly and protect facings of material from extraneous glue.

CAUSTICIZE: To make caustic, especially to convert an alkaline carbonate into a hydroxide by the use of lime.

CAUSTICIZER: Tanks used to convert spent liquor and lime hydrate into hydroxide.

CHAFER: A strip of rubberized fabric that covers bead section of tire to protect plies, which cover bead, from rubbing against metal rim of wheel.

CHAIN SAW: A saw made of endless, roller-link chain with saw tooth cut in each link.

CHAIR CLAMP: See CLAMP MACHINE.

CHARACTER: Any symbol, such as a digit or letter that is stored or processed by a COMPUTER.

CHARGER: A cylinder, open at both ends, which is inserted in top of hogshead to extend height of hogshead for packing purposes.

CHARGING MANIFOLD: A hollow pipe fixture containing holes which receive and hold capillary tubes of thermostat bellows while they are being filled with gas.

CHEESE: A yarn package on which many short lengths of yarn have been combined into one continuous strand for more efficient use on machines, such as warpers or twisters.

CHEESE TRIER: A long U-shaped cutting knife used by graders to remove sample plug from cheese block.

CHILL-PROOF: To stabilize or eliminate protein compounds in beer to prolong shelf life.

CHOKER: A noose of wire rope hitched about a log by means of which log is dragged or skidded overground.

CHUCKING MACHINE: A type of single- or multiple-spindle lathe equipped to hold individual workpieces in chucks.

CIAIO: A type of counter-forming liquid which hardens when dry to give rigidity to back of shoe.

CINCO BALANCE TESTER: Equipment for determining moisture content of substances, consisting of infrared drying oven and balance scale graduated to show percentage of moisture and solids.

CLAMP MACHINE: A stationary hand-powered or air-driven vise used to force together and hold joints of wooden assemblies in position while being reinforced by nails, screws, staples, and glue. Also known as CASE CLAMP, CHAIR CLAMP, or BED CLAMP, depending on design or purpose.

CLAMSHELL DREDGE: A heavy steel bucket, divided into two parts hinged at top, fitted to derrick and controlled by cables. It is used to dig earth and gravel in construction work.

CLARIFIERS: A machine having submerged, rotating arms with plow blades which scrape settled silt from bottom of settling basin spirally toward center of machine where silt is collected in trough and sluiced through pipes back to river. The clarifier does not clarify in the usual sense; silt is settled by gravity.

CLEARER ROLLER: A small cloth or felt covered roller driven by frictional contact with rollers to keep rolls clean and collect ROVING waste when end breaks.

CLOSURE: The rubber part with hole containing threads to receive screw-in cap for sealing water bottle.

CLOTH BEAM: A spool 4 to 6 feet long on which cloth is wound as it is produced on loom.

CODE: (I) A system of symbols for representing data or instructions in a COMPUTER or a tabulating machine.

——(II) To translate the PROGRAM for the solution of a problem on a given COMPUTER into a sequence of MACHINE LANGUAGE or PSEUDO INSTRUCTIONS and addresses acceptable to that COMPUTER.

COILER HEAD: An attachment on textile machines that coils SLIVER after it has been processed.

COIL FORM: Paper or plastic tube onto which wire coils are wound. Forms vary in length according to number of coils wound on each form. Multiple wound coil forms are cut on bandsaw into individual coils for assembly into electronic equipment.

COMB: Precut undipped pasteboard resembling a hair comb, used for book matches.

COMBER BOARD: Board extending full width of warp and located above warp threads. It is pierced with small holes and serves to keep harness cords in order, one passing through each hole.

COMMUTATOR HUB: Metal structure used to support a commutator.

COMPUTER: An electronic device capable of accepting information, performing mathematical and logical operations on it, and reporting the results—all under control of a stored PROGRAM.

CONE: A tapered cardboard on which thread or yarn is wound.

CONES: A set of small triangular pyramids of clay mixtures and fluxes so graded that they represent series of fusion points. The degree of heat is measured in kiln by observing which of various cones have bent over.

CONFIGURATION: A group of machines which are interconnected and are programed to operate as a system.

CONSOLE: A portion of the COMPUTER which may be used to control the machine manually, correct errors, determine the status of machine circuits, registers, and counters, determine the contents of STORAGE, and manually revise the contents of STORAGE.

CONSTANT: A fixed or invariable value or data item.

CONTACT PROCESS: Catalytic method of producing sulfuric acid by treatment of sulfur dioxide with catalytic agents and reaction of resulting product with water in absorbing towers.

CONTINUOUS MINER: An electric hydraulically operated machine that cuts, loads, and conveys coal from coal seams onto belt conveyors or shuttle cars.

CONTROL PAPER: A narrow ribbon of paper that is perforated by operation of keyboard to correspond to various sizes and styles of type. The perforated ribbon is then inserted in another machine wherein compressed air passing through perforations performs selection of matrices and casting of type metal in the matrices.

COOLANT: A liquid used to cool, lubricate, and wash cutting tool and workpiece contact area during machining. Also known as cutting fluid.

COP: A paper tube on which yarn is wound; also quantity of yarn wound on a cop.

CORDEDGE: A strip of bias-cut cloth folded over cord and sewn to form trimming used in edging wearing apparel.

COUNTERBORING: A machining process in which an enlarged, flat-bottomed cylindrical hole is made at opening of existing hole usually so that bolt head or nut can be seated flush with or below surface.

COUNTING GLASS: A small magnifying glass mounted over square inch frame used to count mesh of wire cloth.

COVER MAT: A square or rectangular mat formed by stapling two thicknesses of veneer staves together. Mats are subsequently cut into circular basket covers or lids.

CRACKS: The outer grooves cut in buhr stones.

CREEL: A rack holding spools or CHEESES from which yarn is drawn in weaving.

CRIB: A large raft of logs with wire rope interwoven between logs to add strength for ocean travel. Sometimes known as Davis Raft.

CRIMPING ATTACHMENT: Two feed rolls and a stuffer box into which yarn is overfed, then folded or bent at a sharp angle and then heat-set during compression by attached heating element.

CRYSTALLOGRAPHIC AXIS: One or more lines of reference intersecting at center of a crystal to determine crystal system to which crystal belongs.

CUP: Similar to SPREADER PAN in which it sets. Spreads molten lead around spreader pan through holes in side. Receives lead as it comes from spout.

CURING OVEN: A loop or roller-type drier through which resin treated fabrics are run in open width at high temperature to convert soluble resin into insoluble compound.

CUTLINES: Outlines of shapes of glass to be followed for cutting and leading stained-glass windows.

CUTTER CHANGE POINT: A point, expressed in three dimensional coordinates, at which cutting tool of automatic machine tool changes direction.

CUTTER HEAD: A rotating tool holder into which blades are clamped. It is used in machine tools in which rotating cutting tools are employed.

CYLINDER SCALE: Same as FAN SCALE, except the reading face is essentially a rotatable cylinder on horizontal axis.

CYSTOSCOPE: Instrument for interior examination of bladder.

DATA PROCESSING: (I) The preparation of source media which contain data or basic elements of information, and the handling of such data according to precise rules of procedure to accomplish such operations as classifying, sorting, calculating, summarizing, and recording.

——(II) The production of records and reports.

DEBUG: To diagnose and correct computer malfunctioning or mistakes in programing.

DECANTER: A rectangular, steel tank in which tar and ammonia are separated by settling according to their differences in specific gravity.

DENSIMETER: A machine that measures density or specific gravity of rubber samples by indicating on dial the maximum amount of air pressure which can be applied to it. (The lesser the amount of pressure, the greater the density.)

DENT: The space between two wires in reed of loom.

DEPHLEGMATOR: A fractionating column attached to a still in which vapor from the still is partially condensed, liquifying a portion of the vapor which is richer in the higher boiling constituents than the original vapor. The condensate may be returned to the still to enrich the vapor coming from it.

DEVULCANIZER: A machine used in treating ground scrap rubber with chemicals and steam to restore it as near as possible to its original physical and chemical state for use as RECLAIM rubber.

DIAGRAM: (I) A schematic representation of a sequence of SUBROUTINES designed to solve a problem.

——(II) A coarser and less symbolic representation than a FLOW CHART, frequently including descriptions in English words.

——(III) A schematic or logical drawing showing the electrical circuit or logical arrangements within a component.

DIAL: A flat circular plate that rotates and presents parts to machine at prescribed intervals. The worker places parts on designated spots on dial.

DIAL INDICATOR: A measuring instrument consisting of a feeler point and a clocklike dial. Also known as INDICATING GAGE.

DIGITAL COMPUTER: A COMPUTER which processes information represented by combinations of discrete or

discontinuous data as compared with ANALOG COM-
PUTER for continuous data.

DIPPER DREDGE: A floating dredging machine that excavates by means of a single bucket or dipper on an arm and boom.

DOBBER: A device with serrated edge which separates strands of yarn and keeps them parallel.

DOBBY LOOM: A loom usually used for weaving goods of a nonfloral pattern in which the interlacings are complicated.

DOCTOR: A scraper blade that removes excess material from a roller or from sheet material that passes through the rollers. Also known as doctor blade.

DOG: (I) A piece of metal secured to a base or stationary object against which wedges are driven to move large component parts into specified alinement during an assembly or erection operation.

—— (II) A steel, toothlike projection, several of which are attached to a carriage knee and operated by a lever. They are used to secure the log to the carriage.

DONKEY WATCH: A tour of duty on board ship when at dock to watch over auxiliary engines furnishing steam, light, and power.

DOWN TIME: The period during which a COMPUTER is malfunctioning or not operating correctly due to mechanical or electronic failure as opposed to available time, idle time, or standby time during which the COMPUTER is functional.

DRAFT: The extent to which fibers are lengthened by roving. A draft of five means that the fibers have been drawn to five times their original length.

DRAWING-IN: In weaving, the process of drawing the warp threads from the warp beams through the specified HEDDLE.

DRAWING-IN DRAFT: In weaving, a plan prepared on design paper showing how warp threads are to be drawn through the HEDDLE to produce desired pattern. A drawing-in draft is prepared for all fancy patterns.

DRAWING-IN FRAME: A rack on which harnesses are hung while warp ends are being drawn through HEDDLE eyes.

DRIFT PIN: A tapered steel pin for alining rivet holes before inserting the rivet.

DRIP: A tank located below level of gas mains, and connected to main by pipes, for the purpose of collecting condensed water, gas, and tars which must be drained from the main continually to prevent congestion and eventual rupture of the pipe. Capacities of the tanks vary from a few gallons to as much as 500 gallons.

DRIVEMATIC RIVETING MACHINE: A machine equipped with work positioner and tape control that automatically performs drilling, countersinking, dimpling, and riveting operations on aircraft wing panels and fuselage sections.

DROP WIRE: In textile machines, thin metal strip with an eye through which single strands of yarn are passed. If the yarn breaks, the wire drops to cut the electric circuit, thus stopping the machine.

DRYING CANS: A machine used in textile mills to dry fabrics. Several large heated drums, wide enough to accommodate one or two widths of cloth, are arranged in tiers. Cloth threaded through drums contact a large area of each and are rapidly dried.

DUMPING PIVOT: A simple steel basket open at top and one side to accommodate ice freezing containers. The lower corner opposite open side is hinged to facilitate tipping and removal of ice block.

DUROMETER: A device that measures hardness of cured rubber stock by recording on a dial indicator the depth of impression a spring-loaded button can make at specified pounds pressure.

DWELL METER: An electrical meter used to measure dwell or time interval between closing cycle of distributor points of automobile ignition system. Incorrect spacing of points results in improper dwell.

EDGER: A machine that automatically cuts dovetail tongues and grooves in opposing lengthwise edges of boards, applies glue to the formed edges, and interlocks the tongues and grooves of adjoining boards to form panels. Also known as LINDERMAN MACHINE.

ELECTRONIC DATA PROCESSING: DATA PROCESSING performed largely by electronic equipment.

ELECTRONIC DATA-PROCESSING EQUIPMENT: See AUTOMATIC DATA-PROCESSING EQUIPMENT.

ELECTRONIC DATA-PROCESSING SYSTEM: The general term used to define a system for DATA PROCESSING by means of machines utilizing electronic

circuitry at electronic speed as opposed to electromechanical equipment.

ENGINE LATHE: The basic type of metal-machining lathe or turning machine, consisting essentially of a bed with a headstock and gearbox on one end, a tailstock (no turret) at the other, and a carriage, cross-slide, and toolpost in between.

ERROR: The extent to which precision is lost in a given quantity or the difference between a quantity and its calculated approximation.

EXTENDER: A white inert substance added to pigments and dyes to reduce color strength or give more body.

EXTRACTOR: A device used to extract water from fabrics, knit goods, or other materials by whirling them within a rotating perforated drum at high speed; a centrifuge.

EYELET PLATE: A crossbar attached to CREEL immediately in front of each row of spindles, perforated with same number of holes as there are spindles, that guide individual ends from packages on spindles to loom.

FACING: A machining operation that is a form of turning in which the tool is fed at right angles to axis of workpiece rotation to produce flat surface.

FAKING DOWN: A method of coiling and laying ropes, nets, and other linear materials in overlapping figure 8's so they will run out without tangling when pulled at one end.

FALLER: A narrow metal bar set with one or more rows of sharp, pointed pins that comb through sliver to blend and aline fibers.

FALLER WIRE: A device on a mule-spinning frame to keep yarn under tension during winding and to guide it onto bobbins.

FALSE SELVAGE: An extra layer of selvage woven on each edge of some looped pile fabrics. This selvage is formed by FLOATS inserted to hold loop pile during weaving. Both false selvage and floats are removed after cloth is doffed from loom.

FALSE-TWIST SPINDLE: A hollow spindle with small wheel mounted in its aperture used in manufacture of stretch yarn. Yarn processed through this spindle is commonly referred to as false-twisted yarn.

FAN SCALE: An automatic indicating scale, usually price-computing counter scale, whose reading face is a fan chart.

FEASIBILITY STUDY: A study undertaken to identify various areas of operation within an organization which appear to be susceptible to AUTOMATIC DATA PROCESSING so as to determine the possible impact of ADP within these areas in terms of operating economies or improved management efficiency.

FEATHERS: Strips of metal, flat on one side and curved on the other, used in pairs with wedge between to split stone.

FEED CUPS: Feeding mechanism on sewing machine on which needle operates horizontally. Two wheels or discs which rotate in horizontal plane to pull material between them.

FEED DOG: Knurled metal piece that intermittently feeds fabric material beneath needle of sewing machine.

FEEDER TUBE: A clay tube clamped in orifice of FOREHEARTH to capture and hold gob of molten glass for delivery to bottlemaking machines.

FELL: The edge of cloth nearest to reed as it is being woven in loom; consequently, the last few PICKS which shuttle has drawn through.

FELLING STITCH: A sewing stitch that does not completely penetrate material in which it is made. Such stitching is used to fasten lining into garments so that stitches do not show on outside.

FERRULE: A threaded metal ring to receive screw-in cap for sealing ice bag.

FESTOONS: Two banks of evenly spaced rollers in four-roll calender used for accumulating fabric to maintain continuous operations while making roll changes and for taking up slack in fabric prior to calendering.

FILING JIG: A jig inserted in recessed area of wooden gunstock to facilitate filing, sanding, or scraping of adjacent areas.

FILLER: The tobacco used for the interior portion of cigars, chewing (plug and twist) and plug smoking tobacco.

FILLING: The cross threads in woven fabric that pass over and under the warp threads.

FILLING BOBBIN: A tapered spindle on which FILLING is wound. It is held in battery of loom from where it is automatically injected into shuttle when needed.

FILLING PILE FABRIC: Fabric in which an extra set of filling yarns forms pile. Examples are corduroy and velveteen.

FILM: A thin layer of light-sensitive silver emulsion applied to plates, films, and papers; a photographic material comprising sensitive layer on transparent flexible support; an image on photographic film; the thin skinlike collodion image after removal from its temporary glass or flexible support.

FILTER AID: A substance, such as diatomaceous earth, used to increase effectiveness of filtration equipment.

FILTRACELL: A siliceous material that absorbs impurities and clarifies oil pressed from corn GERMS.

FILTROSE: A catalytic agent used in production of butadiene.

FINDINGS: (I) A term applied to miscellaneous fittings, such as buttons, snaps, eyes, and ornaments that are sewed or otherwise attached to garments and shoes during manufacture.

—— (II) A term applied to unassembled parts of jewelry, such as links, enameled pieces, pin stems, catches, joints, earring clips, and necklace clasps.

FINGER BUFF: Strips of buffing cloth used in manufacture of buffing wheels. These strips are attached to core of buffing wheel with LACING and form fingerlike projections.

FINISH: A starchy compound applied to fabric to give it body.

FIRED POTTERY: Pottery that has been baked in an oven or kiln.

FIXED BRIDGE: A dental appliance that is permanently attached to natural teeth or roots which furnish primary support.

FIXTURE: See JIG AND FIXTURE.

FLAGGING: Dried strips of a marsh weed, such as cattail.

FLASH: The ridge or line of excess material left on metal or plastic objects along the parting or closing line of mold. Also known as fin.

FLAT: One of many lattices in chain covered with fine wire and used on CARDING MACHINE to comb fibers parallel.

FLIGHT FOLLOWING BOARD: A board fastened to wall, ruled vertically and horizontally forming rectangular grid spaces, and used to post flight number, airplane number, and arrival times of flights.

FLITCH: A four-sided section of log from which veneer strips are sliced.

FLOATS: The portion of warp or FILLING yarn that extends over two or more adjacent strands of warp threads or filling PICKS to form design during weaving; or that passes through loops of looped pile fabric, such as corduroy, to hold loops in position during weaving.

FLOORS: The concentric grooves cut near the center of buhr stone.

FLOW CHART: Synonymous with process chart and flow DIAGRAM. A graphic representation of the major steps of work in process. The illustrative symbols may represent documents, machines, or actions taken during the process.

FLOUR-ROLL CALENDER: A machine which coats both sides of fabric stock with rubber simultaneously and rolls sheets to specifications.

FLOWER NAIL: A long nail with large head that is used as base to create intricate designs with icings.

FLOWMETER: An instrument for indicating pressure, velocity of flow, and rate of discharge of gas or vapor (such as steam) flowing in pipe. Usually equipped with recording pen and chart.

FLUSHED COLOR: A pigment from which water has been displaced by another liquid such as oil. Most of the water is drawn off top and the rest is removed by vacuum.

FLYER: An inverted, U-shaped metal arm that twists the ROVING or sliver and guides it on the bobbin.

FONT: A complete set of photomatrices which may be made up of individual photomats for each character or all may be combined on a single plate or filmstrip.

FOREHEARTH: A tunnellike structure of fired brick which receives molten glass from melting furnace and maintains it at uniform temperature for delivery to bottlemaking machines.

FORM BOARD: A specified number of FORM STRIPS fastened together side by side with long bolts.

FORMER: A machine used to twist roving or yarn into strands to make rope.

FORMING CHUCK: A metal block shaped to contour and attached to machine spindle which serves dual purpose of holding and rotating cylindrical workpieces and as forming die to shape workpiece to contour.

FORM STRIP: An aluminum strip to which forms for dipping such items as balloons and gloves into latex are fastened.

FORM TOOL: A cutting tool ground to specific contour in order to machine the inverse contour in workpiece.

FORTRAN: A programing language designed for problems which can be expressed in algebraic notation, allowing for exponentation and up to three subscripts.

FOTO MAT: Linotype metal matrices with small film of letter in center.

FOUR-ROLL CALENDER: A machine which coats both sides of fabric stock with rubber simultaneously and rolls sheets to specifications. Also known as Z-CALENDER.

FOXING: A strip of uncured rubber or rubber-coated fabric placed around footwear at juncture of sole and upper to hold them together, improve appearance, and waterproof article.

FRACTIONATOR: A conical centrifuge used to isolate proteins from whole blood plasma in production of drugs. Plasma is diluted with alcohol to increase its acidity and centrifuge, causing protein to settle to bottom.

FRAMING TIMBERS: To cut, trim, notch, bore, and shape wood products, such as poles, trusses, spans, stringers, and ties.

FRAZING MACHINE: A machine which guides briar block against cutters to duplicate preselected pipe shape. A clamp-fitted shaft and a cam follows a master model to shape shank and lower half of bowl.

FREENESS: The quality of pulp stock that determines rate at which it parts with water when being formed into sheet on wire screen or perforated plate. The same quality is known as freeness, slowness, or wetness according to type of instrument used to estimate it.

FRENCH BINDING: A narrow strip of fabric that is stitched to edge of shoe uppers and folded over to form smooth finished edge.

FRENOTOMY: Cutting of mucous membrane under tongue.

FROTHING MACHINE: A mixing machine with electrically operated agitating paddles used for mixing air with latex to obtain desired density.

FULLING MILL: A machine that shrinks and felts fibers of woolen cloth through application of moisture, heat, friction, and pressure. May be used to crush and dust carbonized vegetable matter from dry woolen cloth.

FURNISH: The mixture of various materials, such as pulp, sizing, fillers, and dyes, from which paper is made.

FUR MACHINE: A special type of machine that sews leather or skins of fur with chain stitch. The material moves sideways, instead of away from the operator.

GAGE BLOCKS: Hardened steel blocks, each of a standard dimension, used as standards in precision measuring. Sometimes referred to by trade names, as JOHANSSON BLOCKS, or (in shop usage) JO-BLOCKS.

GAMB STICK: A metal or wooden rod with pointed or hooked ends which are inserted through the tendons on the hind legs of animal carcass to hold the legs apart while animal is dressed. The stick has a rind in the center for attaching to a trolley or an overhead rail.

GANG KNIFE: A set of knives, arranged to be raised and lowered by hand, used to slice fish into several pieces of predetermined length.

GANGSAW: A number of circular saws keyed to one shaft to perform several cutting operations simultaneously.

GARNETT MACHINE: A machine similar to a CARDING MACHINE, used to open hard-twisted yarn wastes, rags, and clippings. Cylinders are covered with coarse wire teeth.

GAS CHECK: A metal cup, coated with oil or wax, that expands to form a gastight, moving seal under piston of device used to measure pressure produced within gun barrel by exploding cartridge.

GEAR CAGES: A cluster of gears, bearings, and locking devices usually attached to a shaft.

GEAR GENERATING: A gear-machining operation in which the cutter teeth have (or simulate) the shape of mating gear teeth rather than of the space between the teeth, and the cutting is done as the cutter and gear blank rotate together.

GEL: A heavy fluid containing solid materials, such as round-grained sand, walnut hulls, or aluminum

pellets, and used, along with pressure, to fracture gas or oil-bearing rock formations.

GERM: A term sometimes applied to the embryo which occurs in seed plants immediately after fertilization and then undergoes a resting period in the seed until germination takes place.

GIMP THREAD: Heavy twinelike thread used to reinforce edges of buttonholes in heavier garments.

GORE: An elastic insert in side, front, or panels of a shoe used to decorate or reinforce, or to allow stretching that will provide additional comfort and freedom of movement to wearer.

GREIGE: Untreated textile fabric as it comes from the loom or knitting machine, so called because of its gray, unfinished appearance.

GRIZZLY: A device consisting of a group of strong iron bars or revolving disks used to size broken rock or coal.

GROUND TACKLE: The anchors, cable, and other gear used to secure a vessel at anchor or dock.

HALF LAP: Approximately half of a hollow, cylindrical shell on which are fastened 17 brass bars set with steel needles. The size of the needles and their spacing varies from bar to bar.

HALFTONE CUT: A printed impression made from halftone plate.

HAMMER MILL: A grinding mill that breaks up particles of material by impact of whirling bars (hammers) attached to rapidly rotating hub.

HAND: (I) The feel of textile goods as soft, harsh, smooth, rough, boardy.

—— (II) A bundle of tobacco leaves tied together at the stem ends, usually with a tie leaf of tobacco.

HARNESS FRAME: Two wooden laths upon which are suspended series of cords or wires called HEDDLES.

HARP: Metal frame crossed horizontally or vertically with fine cutting wire to cut curd (coagulated or thickened part of milk) in vat or kettle to measured size.

HEADER: A fabricated chamber to which series of tubes are joined to permit free circulation of fluid within water tube boiler.

HEDDLE: A fiber or metal strand on HARNESS FRAME of loom through which warp threads pass.

HIGH-LEAD RIG: Any of several logging systems that utilize one or more tall spar trees with main operating line running from top of spar outward over yarding area.

HOB: A gear-cutting tool shaped like worm whose threads are interrupted with grooves to form series of cutting teeth.

HOBBING: A gear-machining operation in which teeth are generated by rotating HOB and gear blank against each other with action similar to that of worm gear. See GEAR GENERATING.

HOG MILL: A power-driven machine for cutting scrap wood into fine particles suitable for blowing as fuel into fireboxes or boilers with compressed-air jet.

HOOKER MACHINE: A machine that folds cloth by means of blade that guides fabric back and forth across surface of table.

HYDROL: A light-brown sirupy liquid formed in manufacture of dextrose.

IMPACT WRENCH: A pneumatic wrench used to tighten or loosen nuts and bolts.

INDEXING: Moving workpiece or toolholding device, such as a turret, to a series of regularly spaced positions to repeat an operation or to perform a series of operations at predetermined intervals.

INDICATING GAGE: See DIAL INDICATOR.

INPUT: Information transferred from auxiliary or external STORAGE into internal STORAGE.

INSTRUCTION: A set of COMPUTER WORDS or CHARACTERS that define the operation to be performed by a COMPUTER.

INVEST: To cover, envelop, or surround wholly or in part an object, such as denture, tooth, wax form, crown, etc., with heat-resisting material (refractory material) before curing, soldering, or casting.

INVESTMENT: A pastelike material used to maintain positions of metal parts during soldering or welding.

INVOLUTE CHECKER: A device for inspecting involute curves on teeth of gears, splines, etc.

JACQUARD LOOM: Loom equipped with device for weaving figured fabrics. The Jacquard attachment consists of mechanism controlled by perforated cards which cause warp threads to be lifted in proper succession for producing figure.

J-BOX: A vertical tunnel or container, shaped like letter

J, used in wet-cloth finishing operations to make process continuous.

JIG AND FIXTURE: Frequently the terms "jig" and "fixture" are used interchangeably. More precisely, jig is defined as a device that holds work in position and also guides tools acting upon the work; while fixture is considered as a clamping device with no provision for guiding tools.

JIGGER: Small pointed metal instrument, resembling sharpened pencil, used in assembling ribs of expansion metal watch bands.

JO-BLOCKS: See GAGE BLOCKS.

JOHANSSON BLOCKS: See GAGE BLOCKS.

JOLLY: An apparatus similar to a jigger by which plastic clay is formed into pottery, such as cups, urns, and planters. The shaping tool, suspended from cable with pulley and counterweight in upright support, shapes inside of ware.

JUMP IRON: A heavy iron, supported by movable arm, designed to eject steam through holes in bottom. A pedal is depressed to lower iron and to apply pressure to article being pressed. The iron is pushed back and forth manually.

KAPLAN: A control for water turbines which varies pitch of blades in accordance with load, resulting in high efficiency over large-load range.

KNOTTER: A device that ties two threads and clips off loose ends in one operation. May be strapped to hand or around waist. On automatic spoolers or winders knotter is part of machine and yarn is drawn into knotter by vacuum.

LACING: A circular metal strip with serrated edges used in manufacture of buffing wheels to secure buffing material to center of wheel. The serrated edges are bent outward to form groove in which material is inserted.

LADDER DREDGE: A floating dredging machine that excavates by means of a series of buckets on endless chain.

LAG BOLT: A lag screw; a screw with wood-screw threads on one end and tap-screw threads or wrench head on other end.

LAP: (I) A tool, usually of softer material than workpiece and of complementary shape, which is charged with LAPPING COMPOUND. See LAPPING.

—— (II) A roll of loosely matted cotton fiber.

—— (III) A horizontal wheel or disk made of cast iron, used to fine-grind flat surfaces on diamonds or other stones.

LAPPING: Smoothing, finishing, or achieving an extremely close tolerance (e.g., 0.000002 inch in gage block manufacture) on metal surface by means of a LAP that is charged with LAPPING COMPOUND and rubbed against workpiece in rotary and/or reciprocating motion, either by hand or machine. Matching workpieces may be lapped against each other to assure a close fit. Sometimes used loosely to denote fine grinding or honing.

LAPPING COMPOUND: A fine abrasive flour, usually mixed with oil, water, or some other vehicle in the form of paste, which becomes imbedded or "charged" in the LAP. See LAPPING.

LAP-UPS: A term used in textile industry denoting material (lap, thread, fibers, etc.) which becomes entangled in or wound about machinery.

LASER (Light Amplification by Stimulated Emission of Radiation): A device in which chromium atoms are excited by intermittent flashes of light, causing them to emit radiation in form of light. This radiation is in turn amplified by mirrored ends of atom emitter.

LASTING: The operation of tacking a shoe upper and insole to a last or of turning down and sticking together the upper and sole of rubber footwear by hand or machine.

LASTING TOOL: A combination handtool usually composed of hammerhead, pincers, and tack puller used in construction of shoes. Also known as lasting pincers or shoemaker's pliers.

LATCH NEEDLE: A knitting-machine needle, the hook of which can be closed by a latch pinned to shank of needle. When latch is closed, the needle, carrying yarn, may be drawn through loop to form a chainstitch.

LATCH-UP NEEDLE: A NEEDLE used for hand mending dropped stitches or runs in hosiery or knitted garments.

LAUTERTUB: A closed, insulated tank containing cutting-raking device, metal filter, and sprinkling device used in beer manufacture to withdraw clear wort from grain mash.

LAY: A number of layers of material, each layer being placed on the layer beneath, with corners and edges in coincidence.

LAYBOY: An automatic mechanism that receives, stacks, and jogs sheets of paper into piles. It may be attached to machines, such as cutters, printing presses, or ruling machines. Generally equipped with counting and tabbing devices.

LEACH TANK: A tank containing hot water into which uncured balloons are dipped to remove bitter taste of coagulant.

LEADER: A piece of fabric or other material, attached to one end of cloth or yarn that serves to pull and guide it through a machine at the beginning of the operation.

LEAD WIRES: Soft metal wires used to take impressions between two adjoining parts to determine clearances measured by micrometers.

LEASE: The method of arranging and retaining strands and skeins in an orderly fashion to prevent tangling during processing and weaving.

LEASE ROD: A long oval rod, usually of wood, inserted between the threads of a warp to form a LEASE.

LEASE STRING: Strings inserted between the threads of a warp to hold the threads in the same relative position for drawing-in or tying to old warp.

LEHR: An enclosed tunnellike oven containing heating and cooling elements through which materials such as glass are conveyed for heat-conditioning and slowly and evenly cooled to eliminate internal stresses.

LETOFF RACK: A rack that operates with braking action permitting machine to pull material from a roll.

LET-OUT PELT: Fur pelt cut into diagonal strips and resewn to make pelt longer and narrower and to improve its quality and appearance.

LEVER: In a scale, a part provided with pivots or plate fulcrums for translating external forces.

LIGHT TABLE: A table or bench having translucent top over a light source. It is used in examining objects where it is desired that no shadow will be cast.

LINDERMAN MACHINE: *See* EDGER.

LITE: Flat glass cut to specified size from continuous sheet of glass.

LITHOGRAPHIC STONE: A fine-grained, porous limestone on which designs are transferred for lithographic printing.

LOADING BOX: A receptacle, usually part of or rigidly attached to a lever into which molten metal or equivalent may be poured to aid in balancing scale under a zero load.

LOOM BEAM: A large wood or metal cylinder, 4 to 6 feet long, on which are wound the warp threads for a loom.

LOOPER: Part of mechanism of sewing machine that forms loop in thread, through which needle passes to make a lockstitch.

LOOPING LINE: A line of stitches knitted into both sides of the open toe of seamless hose as a guide along which the looper must set the stitches to produce a straight looped toe.

LOOPING MACHINE: (I) A machine that forces ends of helical springs around die to form a hook so that springs can be linked to other bedspring parts.

—— (II) A machine that knits two parts of knitted garment or stocking together.

LOUPE: A magnifying glass.

LUMITE: A liquid which hardens when dry to give rigidity to back of shoe.

MACHINE LANGUAGE: *See* MACHINE ORIENTED LANGUAGE.

MACHINE ORIENTED LANGUAGE: (I) A language designed for interpretation and use by a machine without translation.

—— (II) A system for expressing information which is intelligible to a specific machine, e.g., a COMPUTER or class of COMPUTERS. Such a language may include instructions which define and direct machine operations and information to be recorded by or acted upon by these machine operations.

MAGNETIC TAPE: A continuous flexible recording medium whose base material is impregnated or coated with a magnetic sensitive material ready to accept data in the form of magnetically polarized spots.

MAKE-OVER: In newspaper work, subject matter that is to replace copy on newspaper pages to make a new edition.

MASER (Microwave Amplification by Stimulated Emission of Radiation): A device which subjects molecules or atoms of a paramagnetic material to a microwave signal which triggers release of radiation.

MASTER: Copper negative electroplate made by electrodeposition on original lacquer recording disk on which a record has been made. Required in making STAMPER, which presses positive of recording into phonograph records.

MASTER STRAIGHTEDGE: A straight slender bar made of rigid material, which is placed across wide points of contact to hold the level on a structure to be leveled.

MAT BOARD: A cardboard material with a dull finish on one side, used for picture borders. It is prepared in white and tinted finishes.

MATHEMATICAL MODEL: The general characterization of a process, object, or concept, in terms of mathematics, which enables the relatively simple manipulation of variables to be accomplished in order to determine how the process, object, or concept would behave in different situations.

MEASURING WIRES: Accurately made short wires of standard diameters, for use in precision measuring of gear or thread dimensions.

MECHANICAL PRINT: An engineering drawing that is the actual pictorial presentation of a product, part, or machine, showing dimensions, type of material, wiring, and other details.

MEGGER: An instrument used to measure insulation resistance or electrical resistance of electrical equipment, such as powerline poles.

MEMORY: *See* STORAGE.

MENDING DISK: An electrically powered mending device containing wire or plastic fingers that revolve rapidly to pull picked or pulled threads into position on hose.

METALWORK: The skeletal portion of a dental appliance around which and to which are attached the remaining portions of the appliance to produce the finished unit.

MILANESE FABRIC: A highly run-resistant knitted fabric in which the yarn runs diagonally across the face of fabric. The fabric is usually made into gloves and underwear.

MILIEU THERAPY: Method of treatment in which interaction of patient and environment are utilized.

MILL: A small, soft-steel cylinder upon surface of which a design in relief is made by rolling in contact with die.

MILLING CUTTER: A multiple-toothed or fluted disk or cylinder that shaves the surface of a workpiece as it is rotated in contact with the material.

MINERAL WOOL BLANKET: A continuous ribbon of mineral wool fibers, 2 to 4 inches thick and up to 10 feet wide, that is cut into insulation batts and felts.

MOLD-PRINTING BOARD: The board on which molds are fixed in rows and which, when placed upside down over a tray of leveled starch leaves indentations into which fluid candy is introduced.

MORTAR GUIDE: A metal band that fits the edge of a stone and has a projecting side the thickness of a joint.

MOSS: A form cadmium metal takes when the molten metal drops into cold water. This bubblelike form of solidified metal enhances dissolution.

MOTHER: Nickel positive electroplate made by electrodeposition on MASTER electroplate. Required in making STAMPER, which presses positive of recording into phonograph records.

MUFFLE FURNACE: A closed furnace designed so material may be placed in it, yet not come in direct contact with the fire.

MULTIMETER: A meter used to test electrical or electronic circuits that serves as an ammeter, ohmmeter, voltmeter, and other test meters in a single unit.

NARROWING: The process of contracting size of knit articles, especially a stocking, by taking two stitches in one.

NAUMKEAGING MACHINE: A shoe-buffing machine equipped with an inflated, fine-abrasive pad revolving on upright spindle. Pad is filled with air from compressor attachment of machine.

NECK RING: A cast iron ring which is used in conjunction with mold to form neck of bottle.

NEEDLE: One of a set of parallel slender rods or wires fitted into slotted metal bar used in knitting to hold stitch formed by SINKER II.

NEEDLE BAR: A slotted metal bar in which knitting needles or points are inserted and clamped to plates that hold them in position in knitting machine.

NEEDLE BOARD: A long, narrow board into which are set hundreds of needles to punch bits of felt between threads of burlap or other textile.

NEEDLE JACKS: Small metal pieces, fitted into grooves in needlebed of knitting machine, that transmit reciprocating motion to needles.

NEPS: (I) Little knots in cotton fiber formed by irregular growth of plant or by friction in process machinery.

—— (II) Minute, tangled masses of cotton, wool, or synthetic fibers.

NOTAMS (Notice to Airmen): A notice or report to inform flight crews of hazards in flying and landing aircraft and changes in condition of navigational aids or landing facilities.

NUMERICAL CONTROL: A system of automatic-machine operation in which product specifications are translated into numerical-machine instructions which are recorded on cards or tape (punched or magnetic) and transmitted through control unit to the machine, so that it automatically performs specified operations, often verifying results and making corrective adjustments automatically.

OCCLUSAL HARMONY: The occlusal relationship of opposing teeth in all functional ranges and movements that provides greatest masticatory efficiency without causing undue strain upon supporting tissues.

OFF-LINE: Pertaining to the operation of INPUT-OUTPUT devices or auxiliary equipment not under direct control of the central processing unit.

ON-LINE: Pertaining to the operation of INPUT-OUTPUT devices under direct control of the central processing unit.

OPTICAL FINISH: The quality of surface of lens after scratches and pits have been polished out. The optical finish is determined by inspecting lens under magnifying glass.

OPTICAL FLAT: A tool made from transparent material, such as fused quartz or glass, whose surface is polished to be a true plan within tolerance of millionths of an inch. Used as precise measuring gage of flatness of surfaces by reflection of monochromatic light.

OPTICAL SCANNER: A device that automatically samples or verifies a number of measuring points and indicates those that have drifted from their desired values.

ORDER: To condition tobacco for handling by subjecting it to steam or water.

ORDERING MACHINE: A machine in which tobacco is brought to desired moisture content by application of water or steam spray in cylindrical device or compartment through which conveyor belt passes.

OUTPUT: Information transferred from internal STORAGE to external STORAGE or to an ON-LINE OUTPUT device.

OVERBURDEN: Overlaying earth and rock deposits which cover coal, ore, or rock in strip mine, open pit, or quarry.

PACKAGE DYEING MACHINE: A dyeing machine resembling large pressure cooker. The yarn to be dyed is wound on perforated beams or tubes so that dye solution can be circulated through package.

PAGODA: A removable assembly of cone-shaped steel troughs placed inside a retort to provide greater heating surface for sublimation of magnesium.

PALLET: A metal fixture weighing over 100 pounds that holds workpieces as they are machined in transfer machine. It rides on track from which it is never removed and is lifted into position at each work station by hydraulic pushers.

PALLET STONES: Jewels in pallet of watch which provide a hard, smooth surface on which teeth of escape wheel act.

PAPER TAPE: A strip of paper capable of storing or recording information. STORAGE may be in the form of punched holes, partially punched holes, carbonization or chemical change of impregnated material, or by imprinting. Some PAPER TAPES, such as punched PAPER TAPES, are capable of being READ by the INPUT device of a COMPUTER or a transmitting device by sensing the pattern of holes which represent coded information.

PARAMETER: (I) A quantity in a SUBROUTINE whose value specifies or partly specifies the process to be performed. It may be given different values when the SUBROUTINE is used in different main ROUTINES or in different parts of one main ROUTINE, but usually remains unchanged throughout any one such use.

—— (II) A quantity used in a generator to specify machine CONFIGURATION, designate SUBROUTINES to be included, or otherwise describe the desired ROUTINE to be generated.

PARAMETER: (III) A CONSTANT or a variable in mathematics which remains fixed during some calculation.
— (IV) A definable characteristic of an item, device, or system.

PARTICLE BOARD: Boards made from resin-bonded wood chips used as lumber substitute.

PATCHBOARD: A component of some DATA PROCESSING machines which permits the expression of INSTRUCTIONS in a semifixed COMPUTER PROGRAM by the insertion of pins, plugs, or wires into sockets or hubs in the components in a pattern to represent instructions and thus making electrical interconnections which may be sensed by the DATA PROCESSING machine.

PATTERN CHAIN: The part on textile or sewing machines that controls certain machine actions to produce desired pattern, color, shape, size, or novelty effect. On DOBBY LOOMS and knitting machine, the chain is made of joined metal links or pegs; on JACQUARD LOOMS, it consists of perforated cardboard strips joined by cords; on embroidery machines, it is a perforated strip.

PELLITZER: A revolving pan, about 12 feet in diameter, set on an angle.

PENCIL EDGE: The round or convex surface edge of glass or mirror after edges have been ground. To apply such edge by grinding.

PERIPHERAL EQUIPMENT: The auxiliary machines not under the control of the central COMPUTER.

PICK: (I) One thread of FILLING either before weaving or in cloth. Number of picks per inch of warp is measure of fineness of fabric.
— (II) A short metal rod tapered to a point and mounted in wooden handle, resembling an ice pick, used by wire weavers to pick up and reweave broken wires.

PICK COUNTER: A device containing magnifying lens and pointer, used in counting threads per unit space and in other ways in examining cloth.

PICKING MOTION: The second of three basic motions involved in weaving yarn into cloth. The motion resulting from mechanism of loom that propels shuttle from one side of loom to the other.

PICOT BAR: A bar of knitting machine that holds slender metal rods (picot points) used to knit a row of large, wide stitches (picot stripe) after welt is knitted.

PIECE UP: The joining or union of two or more ends of sliver, slubbing, ROVING, or yarn by twisting or intermingling fiber ends with fingers.

PILE WIRES: Strips of metal that are inserted into SHED of looms to form pile fabrics, such as carpeting.

PIN BRIDGE: Similar to PINGAGE PLATE except that plate is mounted in bridgelike fixture. The plate of cartridges is set in fixture and raised by treadle action against PINGAGE PPLATE.

PINCH CLEAT: A metal cleat that fits around ends of steel bailing straps. When pinched by strapping tool cleat secures ends and keeps strap taut on bale.

PIN GAGE PLATE: A plate containing rows of equidistant free-floating pins. The pins are inserted in cartridges and are pushed up by powder in cartridges, or remain down if any cartridge has been skipped.

PIN JACK: A cast iron pedestal, usually fastened to shoemaker's bench, on which shoe last is placed during processing operations.

PITCHED WORT: Wort (unfermented beer) with added yeast to promote fermentation.

PITCH FINGER: A metal rod mounted over journal of mill that is used to pitch design on mill in register with other portions of design during engraving process.

PLANER GAGE: A work aid consisting of two right-triangle ground metal blocks fastened together to enable user to adjust their outer parallel surfaces to any dimension within a given range by sliding one block on the other.

PLANETARY ACTION: A double mechanical motion in which a tool is rotated on a center, while that center is revolved in another circle at the same time.

PLATE PRESS: A filter press that removes water from gluten.

PLISSÉ: Crepe fabric which is formed by printing caustic soda on cotton cloth. The printed areas shrink causing unprinted areas to blister, forming raised design. Widely used for garments, such as nightwear.

PLUG: Rubber block marked to indicate hat size.

PLUGBOARD: *See* PATCHBOARD.

PLUMBERS "SNAKE": A flexible steel cable or ribbon which is forced through drains and sewers to remove obstructions.

POACHING: Process of removing acid and impurities from nitrocotton prior to processing into explosives.

POINTS: One of a set of parallel slender rods fitted into slotted metal bar used in knitting to form or position stitches or loops.

PONTIC: The suspended tooth of a fixed partial denture that replaces lost natural tooth.

PORCUPINE: A studded, iron ball suspended from cable on electrically controlled drum on the larry.

POTENTIAL DIFFERENCE: A difference in electrical states existing at two points, which causes current to tend to flow between them. It is measured by work done in transferring a unit charge of electricity from one point to the other.

POTEYE: A ring-shaped device through which open cloth is drawn to bunch it longitudinally into ROPE FORM.

POUNCE: (I) To transfer a design through perforated paper stencil by rubbing or striking perforations with bag of powder or charcoal.
— (II) To smooth surface of felt hat with sandpaper.

POWER PRESS: A machine, used in conjunction with dies, for forming, molding, cutting, and shaping of materials under great pressure.

PREFORM RUBBER: Uncured rubber that is precut to provide specific amount of rubber necessary to fill each mold cavity.

PRICKLER ROLL: A large metal roll with sharp protruding pins that puncture rubber-covered belt to remove trapped air.

PRIMING: Pulling prime (mature tobacco leaves) one by one from plants as they mature in field.

PRINTED CIRCUIT BOARD: A conductive pattern reproduced on insulator (usually laminated plastic) used in place of wires in electronic equipment.

PRINTING ROLLER: *See* PRINTING SHELL.

PRINTING SHELL: A large, engraved copper roller used to print designs in color on cloth when mounted in printing machine.

PRODUCTION: Pertaining to work done in manufacture of identical or similar items in relatively large lots or runs, from approximately 100 up to millions of a kind; products are usually standard items and setups are infrequently changed.

PROFILAMETER: An instrument for measuring roughness or smoothness of surface finish of machined parts.

PROGRAM: A plan to be followed to solve a problem or to process data by means of AUTOMATIC DATA-PROCESSING SYSTEM. A PROGRAM usually includes plans for transcribing and coding data as well as for use of results.

PROGRAM MACHINE: A testing device equipped with clocks and mechanism which feeds perforated tape through machine on 24-hour cycles. Perforations permit electrical contacts which open and close relays to discharge cells at prescribed intervals.

PROGRESSIVE DIE: An integrated stamping die made up of several die units or stations through which workpiece is indexed one station at a time for a series of operations. Usually, a continuous strip of sheet metal is fed into press and completely formed workpiece is ejected from other end with each action of press.

PRONGS: Scissorslike tool with three tines, one on one handle and two on other, used for gripping and twisting.

PROOF BOX: A cabinet conditioned by steam to maintain constant humidity and temperature of about 80° F. Leavened dough is enclosed in box to accelerate fermentation of yeast. Also known as dough closet.

PROP WIRE: A thin strip with an eye through which single strands of yarn pass before machines. If yarn breaks, wire drops to cut electric circuit and open electromagnetic clutch, thus stopping machine.

PROVER: A device for passing measured amount of gas or compressed air under constant pressure through gasmeters to test accuracy of meters.

PSEUDO INSTRUCTION: (I) A symbolic representation in a compiler or interpreter.
— (II) A group of characters having the same general form as a COMPUTER INSTRUCTION but never executed by the COMPUTER as an actual INSTRUCTION.

PUG MILL: A machine which mixes plastic clay and delivers it in homogeneous, compact form suitable for making pottery. Frequently mill is equipped with vacuum chamber to remove air from clay.

PULL-TEST MACHINE: A testing device in which pounds of pull, necessary to pull bullet out of cartridge case, are measured.

QUARTERS: The parts of the upper of a shoe that extend from vamp to back.

QUILL: *See* FILLING BOBBIN.

QUILLER: A machine that separates strands of yarn in warp and winds each strand on bobbin or quill.

RACK: (I) The standard unit of measure for lace. It is the amount of lace woven by 1,920 single motions of loom.
— (II) An element of the indicating mechanism, usually mounted vertically, consisting of a straight bar with teeth on one face designed to mesh with those of a pinion, and so attached to lever train that its vertical motion is proportional to the change in applied load.

RADIAL DRILL PRESS: A machine tool used primarily for metal drilling, which consists of central column and horizontal radial arm to which a vertical drilling spindle is attached.

RADIO FIX: Straight-line radio signal or signals on which receiving station takes bearings to determine geographical position. Radio fix is used in both marine and air navigation.

RANGE: An arrangement of machines used to perform a number of yarn- or cloth-processing operations continuously by feeding material to each unit in succession automatically and without interruption.

RASCHEL FABRIC: A fabric produced on raschel-knitting machines which may vary from the sheerest tulle to coarse carpeting, including specialties, such as lace and elastic fabrics.

READ: To copy information from one form of STORAGE to another or to SENSE the meaning of stored information.

RECLAIM: Rubber material recovered from scrap rubber goods by chemical treatment.

REED: One of a number of thin, flat pieces of steel wire between which warp threads are drawn after they pass through the harness of a loom. They push the filling against the fell of the cloth.

REED HOOK: A flat metal tool, similar to crochet hook, used for drawing individual strands of yarn through reed of loom.

REEFER: The refrigerated compartment on a ship in which perishable food is stowed.

REFRACTOMETER: An optical instrument that measures index of refraction of a liquid, from which percentage of sugar, alcohol, salt, or other substances can be determined by comparison with a chart.

REGISTER: Correct relative position of two or more colors when printed from color plates.

REGISTER WHEEL: A large indexed wheel on pantograph or engraving machine. A gross setting on larger register wheel results in precise placement of design on smaller printing roller.

RELIEVING: A machining process in which a FORM TOOL is used to cut teeth for cutting tools to specified contour.

REST-BEER: Beer left in tanks which is drawn off, mixed with other beer, and filtered.

RETAINER: That part of a fixed or removable partial denture which unites abutment tooth with suspended portion of denture.

RIBBON: Thin metal strip or band used for transmitting force, as from the lever system to the cam of a pendulum assembly. Sometimes called a tape.

RICK: A stack of split wood or pole sections measuring 4 feet high, 8 feet long, and 16 inches wide. One rick equals 42⅔ cubic feet.

RIFT: The direction of the plane of fracture in stone along which it can be split most easily.

RING-ROLLING MACHINE: A machine with one or more pairs of arms which revolve away from each other, catch latex at point of dipping, and roll it up the neck forming the ring of balloon.

ROLLING TABLE: A heated press, the upper platen of which lowers and pivots on a shaft, to compress and roll resin impregnated fabrics onto mandrel.

ROLL PICKER: A pneumatic tool which removes lint and trash from spinning and roving frames by winding it on rapidly rotating spindle.

ROPE FORM: The form in which cloth is gathered or bunched into longitudinal folds by being drawn through a ring or series of rings. Some processing is more easily accomplished with cloth in this form.

ROTARY LATHE: A machine for cutting thin sheets of veneer from logs. The log is supported and rotated on horizontal axis as heavy steel knife is fed against its surface to slice thin sheet of wood from circumference.

ROUNDING JACK: A handtool for trimming hat brims. One end of tool is fitted with sharp blade and the other end is shaped to rest on crown of hat. The tool is drawn around hat brim, using crown as guide, to cut off excess material.

ROUTINE: A set of coded INSTRUCTIONS arranged in proper sequence to direct the COMPUTER to perform a desired operation or sequence of operations. A subdivision of a PROGRAM consisting of two or more INSTRUCTIONS that are functionally related; therefore, a PROGRAM.

ROVING: A continuous, soft, slightly twisted strand of fibers. It is the product of a roving frame, is made from sliver, and is used to produce yarn.

ROYAL JELLY: Partially digested honey and pollen spewed by honeybees to feed larval bees. Honeybees place excess amounts of thin substance in the cells of queen bee larvae.

RUN: The performance of one PROGRAM on a COMPUTER, thus the performance of one ROUTINE or several ROUTINES linked so that they form an automatic operating unit, during which manual manipulations by the computer operator are zero or at least minimal.

SARATOGA: A box or hamper used to carry tobacco during various stages of processing.

SASH GANGSAW: A series of heavy saw blades set in metal frame that reciprocates vertically, used to cut several boards simultaneously from log or cant.

SCINTILLATION AND POSITRON SCANNERS: Instruments for measuring physical properties of radium.

SCRAY: A container or rack used to collect sheet material, such as cloth, in folds or pleats for drying or inspection; or to allow for accumulation of goods between machines operating at different speeds to process material in a continuous operation. It also allows additional cloth to be sewed on without stopping machine.

SCREED: A wooden or metal strip, cut to coincide with proposed sectional contour of roadway, used to level fresh concrete or asphalt.

SCREEN: A sheet of glass ruled in fine lines, used in the reproduction of halftones. The screen is inserted in the camera, and divides the photograph into a gridiron of squares or dots. The density of shade or tone of any portion of the halftone is determined by the number of dots per unit area that exist on the halftone.

SEARCHER: A notched metal strip, tooled to 0.0005 inch thickness, used to remove small particles of threads from brass bobbins.

SEED: Crystallized sugar added to supersaturated corn-sugar solution to hasten formation of corn-sugar crystals.

SENSE: To READ the holes punched in a card or tape.

SERGING STITCH: A V-shaped stitch sewn over edge of fabric to prevent raveling.

SET: To widen toe points of saw teeth to cut a kerf wider than thickness of saw blade. The set prevents saw from binding or rubbing in the kerf.

SET POINT: A point in space, expressed in three dimensional coordinates, at which tip of cutting tool of automatic machine is set before the start of machining operations.

SHADOW LINES: Lines on power ripsaw machine table cast by wire hung between light source and table. Used as guides by saw operators in alining boards before they enter the saw.

SHED: The opening in warp threads through which filling passes.

SHEDDING MOTION: The first of three basic motions involved in weaving yarn into cloth. The motion resulting from mechanism of loom that operates harness to separate warp threads and form SHED for passage of shuttle.

SHEETING: *See* SHEET PILING.

SHEET PILING: Long narrow strips of heavy sheet metal that are interlocked and driven into the earth to serve as retaining wall for earth or water during excavation. Also known as SHEETING.

SHEET-PILING DRIVER: A compressed-air or gasoline-powered hammer used to drive sheet piling. It has a U-shaped shoe or striking head that fits over end of pile.

SHELF-LIFE: A term used to denote measurement of life of products in storage or shipment. It is used in connection with beverages (beer) and dry-cell batteries, indicating degree of capacity or usability when put to use.

SHIP'S CRADLE: A framework or platform of timber under bottom of ship, on which it is launched.

SHOOT WIRE: Wires running short way of cloth or screen as woven.

SHOPPING SERVICE: A service paid for by a store and conducted by an outside organization to test, through actual shopping, courtesy, integrity, honesty, and selling ability of establishment's sales and service personnel.

SHOT PAN: A pan, resembling frying pan, with equidistantly spaced holes in bottom through which molten lead is dropped to form shot pellets. Pans are numbered according to size of holes.

SHUTTLE BINDER: A wood or iron lever located at front or back of, and projecting slightly into, the shuttle box. Its purpose is to check force of shuttle as it enters the box.

SHUTTLE BOX: The container at each side of a loom that receives shuttle at the end of its passage.

SIEVE CLOTH: The fabric belts on printing machine which absorb color solutions from color trays and convey it to rollers that print designs on wallpaper.

SINKER: (I) An elevator platform that submerges felt hat cones in tub of hot water to strengthen cohesion of fur fibers.

—— (II) Slender rods in slotted metal bar used in knitting machines to depress loops upon or between needles.

SIPES: Metal strips inserted in grooves of tire molds to impart thread design in cured tires.

SKIRTLIKE UPPER: The sewn-together vamp, quarters, and counter of nonrubber upper of an article of footwear before rubber, composition, or cork sole is put on. The bottom edges of upper are cemented all around, like the hem of a skirt, for bonding with sole.

SLAKED LIME: A chemical combination of calcium, hydrogen, and oxygen formed by combining quicklime and water.

SLIDE: Distance PALLET STONE moves downward on escape wheel tooth after locking in a watch.

SLUBBER: The first fly frame for drawing and twisting slivers to form rovings.

SOFT BOARD: *See* BOARD.

SPACE GAGE: A rectangular metal piece with parallel rows of fine grooves extending across its face, used as a guide for spacing needles in the NEEDLE BAR of a knitting machine.

SPEECH READING: Visual interpretation of speech, from lip movements, facial expressions, and body movements. Also known as lip reading.

SPINNERET: A small cap with very small holes through which a solution is forced, emerging solidified as a fiber.

SPINNING BOX: A device used in rayon manufacturing for piling thread into ring-shaped CAKES. The thread is drawn into spinning box through glass funnel and wound by centrifugal force.

SPOIL PILES: Earth and rock removed from coal, ore, or rock deposit in strip mine, open pit, or quarry.

SPONGE: A powder form of cadmium with a high zinc content.

SPOT-FACING: A machining process in which the area around a hole is milled to smooth, flat surface by application of a rotating tool with cutting edges on its end or face.

SPREADER PAN: A pan, resembling a frying pan, with holes around the side which sets on legs in the SHOT PAN and spreads lead evenly around shot pan.

SPUR CHUCK: A stubby, pronged fork attached to driving spindle of lathe to assist in mounting and centering workpieces.

SPUTTERING: Bombarding metal surface with positive ions to form fine-grained coating on surface.

STAB: A small metal point set in a die used to mark material which is to be sewn.

STAB SETTER: A tool shaped like a hand punch that fits over the STAB. A hammer is used to set STAB in die.

STAKING: The process of making leather soft and pliable, or stretching it to full size. When machines are used, the leather is drawn back and forth between rollers or over a rounded blade.

STAMPER: Negative electroplate made by electrodeposition on MOTHER electroplate. Stampers are used in record presses to press positive of recording into phonograph records.

STANDARD SIZE SYSTEM: A system decreed by Edward II in 1324 that established a variation of one-sixth of an inch in length between half sizes and one-third of an inch in length between whole sizes of shoes.

STARTER: A bacteria used for souring milk or cream in making dairy products, or for promoting fermentation.

STEAM LANCE: A long pipe attached to a steam source, through which steam under pressure is blown into boiler tubes to remove soot and sludge.

STICKERS: Pieces of lumber used in a kiln to provide space for warm air between layers of green lumber, to promote drying.

STIPPLING TOOL: A small block of metal, the under surface of which is covered with small projections. It is used to make multiple indentations in wood by striking top of tool with hammer or mallet.

STIRRUP: A shackle which transmits to a connection load from only one lever.

STONE LAY: A scheme or diagram of type pages as they should be imposed on the stone or table as opposed to how they actually appear on the printed sheet.

STORAGE: (I) The term preferred to MEMORY.

—— (II) Pertaining to a device in which data can be stored and from which it can be obtained at a later time. The means of storing data may be chemical, electrical, or mechanical.

—— (III) A device consisting of electronic, electrostatic, electrical, hardware, or other elements into which data may be entered and from which data may be obtained as desired.

—— (IV) The erasable STORAGE in any given COMPUTER.

STRAPPING TOOL: A hand-operated device that pulls taut strip-steel straps wrapped around a bale and secures ends by pinching a cleat placed around overlapping ends of strap.

STRIKE: A batch of sugar liquor drained from vacuum pans after boiling has created sugar crystals and reduced solution to specified consistency.

STRIKE UP MARKS: Light pencil lines drawn across and at right angles to the junction of two sail cloths and used as guides to sew cloths together.

STUFFING BOX: A small cylindrical box, filled with fibrous material, mounted on the frame of a machine surrounding a piston rod. Its purpose is to make an airtight or steamtight joint.

STUMMEL: The portion of a smoking pipe consisting of the bowl and shank.

SUBROUTINE: (I) The set of INSTRUCTIONS necessary to direct the COMPUTER to carry out a well-defined mathematical or logical operation.

– – (II) A subunit of a ROUTINE. A SUBROUTINE is often written in relative or symbolic coding even when the ROUTINE to which it belongs is not.

—— (III) A portion of a ROUTINE that causes a COMPUTER to carry out a well-defined mathematical or logical operation.

—— (IV) A ROUTINE which is arranged so that control may be transferred to it from a master ROUTINE and so that, at the conclusion of the SUBROUTINE, control reverts to the master ROUTINE. Such a SUBROUTINE is usually called a closed ROUTINE.

—— (V) A single ROUTINE may simultaneously be both a SUBROUTINE with respect to another ROUTINE and as a master ROUTINE with respect to a third. Usually control is transferred to a single SUBROUTINE from more than one place in the master ROUTINE and the reason for using the SUBROUTINE is to avoid having to repeat the same sequence of INSTRUCTIONS in different places in the master ROUTINE.

SUCTION DREDGE: A floating dredging machine that excavates by means of a centrifugal pump and suction tube that draws mud or saturated sand from a channel and discharges it on shore or elsewhere.

SUPER: A section or story of a beehive containing 8 or 10 frames suspended inside on which bees build honeycomb and fill it with honey.

~~SURFACE GAGE: A device for measuring and marking metal parts at precise distances above a plane surface. It consists of a flat-surfaced metal block and a pointed adjustable rod of hardened steel mounted on the block.~~

SURVEYOR: A precision instrument used to make a pencil mark around a tooth indicating its greatest circumference in any one position relative to the vertical.

SWEEPS: A curved piece of plastic or metal that represents a segment of a circle of a known radius. It is used to check accuracy of curves or to draw original curves.

SWING-FOLDING ATTACHMENT: A device, usually attached to the rear of a processing machine, to fold cloth coming from the machine. It consists of a pair of thin parallel rollers mounted between two arms that swing like a pendulum, laying cloth in loose folds.

SWING WEIGHT: The swing weight of a golf club is a measure of the leverage of the club, from beyond a fixed point, applied against the end of the handle. It is the weight felt by the golfer when he swings the club.

TACK: Riding equipment, such as saddle, riding crop, and saddle weights, used by jockey to ride race horse.

TAKEUP ROLL: A roller, operating continuously or intermittently, that winds long lengths of material after it has passed through a machine.

TALKING BOOK: An album of phonograph records containing complete text of book, periodical, or series of articles, for use by blind library patrons.

TAPE CONDENSER: A device that removes web (a sheet of cotton or other fibers) from CARDING MACHINE, divides, and condenses it into roping ready for spinning.

TELESCOPING GAGE: A precision measuring instrument the end of which can be positioned inside hole or opening and expanded to touch walls; interior dimension can then either be read on calibrations of gage or measured with micrometer.

TELETICKETER: An electrical device that transmits and prints transportation routing information on passenger tickets.

TEMPERATURE POTENTIOMETER: A device to take temperature readings at any given point via transmission through thermocouples to reading device. It is equipped with dial to select from which thermocouple (point) to take reading.

TENSION GUIDE: A device used as guide to provide specified tension during winding, coning, sizing, and warping. This device contains fingers, disks, or washers that apply tension.

TENTER FRAME: A machine that dries and stretches cloth to its original width and straightens its weave after a finishing process.

THRUST END ASSEMBLY: The forward end of turbine at which steam enters.

TIMER DRUM: A metal drum containing series of paralleled slots extending around its circumference to hold timing buttons that trip solenoid switches, as drum revolves, to control operation of bottlemaking machine.

TITRATION: The method or process of determining the strength of a solution in terms of the smallest amount of it which will bring about a given reaction with another known substance. Usually the test is accomplished by the use of an indicator (such as litmus) which changes in color when the reaction takes place.

TOE BOARD: The portion of a board on which toe of stocking is shaped.

TOP: An untwisted strand for sliver of long wool or synthetic fibers from which short fibers have been combed. Top is wound into ball form (about 5 to 15 pounds) after combing.

TORQUE CHUCK: A chuck equipped with clutch that slips when under a given tension.

TOW: A large number of continuous synthetic filaments bunched in loose ropelike form with very little twist.

TRACER CONTROL: A system of machine-tool control in which the cutting tool is automatically made to move in precise parallel relationship to a stylus that is held against and moved along edge of a flat template or surface of three-dimensional model. The motion may be mediated mechanically, hydraulically, or electrically, or by a combination of these.

TRACER POINT: A metal rod placed in chuck of master spindle of wood-carving machine, used to follow around the contour of carving pattern.

TRANSFER ARMS: A mechanical fixture on bottle-making machine that automatically grasps and transfers bottles to and from blanking and forming molds.

TRANSFER BAR: A rectangular metal bar used to transfer knitted garment parts from one full-fashioned knitting machine onto NEEDLE BAR of another.

TRANSFER POINT: The needlelike projections on a TRANSFER BAR or TRANSFER RING over which stitches of knitted material are hung when the material is transferred from one machine to another.

TRANSFER RING: A circular metal ring, equipped with vertical needle points, used to transfer knitted material from one machine to another.

TRAVELER: A small free-running metal ring sliding on a bar through which thread passes in other textile machine to impart a twist to the thread.

TRIBOX: Glass enclosed container housing thermometer and hydrometer through which distilled liquor flows, allowing temperature and specific gravity proof of liquor to be measured.

TRIP BUTTONS: Small bolts locked in slots on TIMER DRUMS to trip solenoid switches that start and stop functions of bottlemaking machines.

TRUING: The shaping of grinding wheel for purpose of producing consistent flatness or contour on the ground workpiece. Usually accomplished by application of diamond, abrasive, or hard metal tool.

TRUSS HOOP: A thick iron hoop used to temporarily hold together barrel staves.

TUBE: (I) A hollow cylinder of cardboard on which cloth or yarn is wound for shipment.

—— (II) A common term used in the paper goods industry to indicate that portion of a paper bag without a bottom.

TUNNEL HEADING: That part of tunnel where digging operations are performed.

TURNER TUBES: A device used in turning gloves, with corresponding rods that push the finger tips of the glove into the tube, partially turning it. Turning is completed manually by worker or automatically on machine.

TURNINGS: An article that has been cut to cylindrical shape on lathe.

ULTRASONIC WAVE MACHINE: A machine that removes foreign matter from polished lenses by sound waves.

UNISHANK: A method of shoe construction in which the insole, steel shank, and tuck are incorporated into a single unit.

VERIFIER: A device that automatically compares (verifies) the CHARACTERS on a manual transcription against retranscription.

VOTATOR: Trade name for machine used to cool hot oils and other liquid ingredients to form solidified margarine or shortening, and to impart smooth texture to product.

V-RING: Rings that are assembled to each end of the commutator, pressed together, and bolted or screwed to the hub of the armature to keep the copper bars in alinement.

WARP WIRE: Wires running the long way of the cloth or screen as woven.

WEASANDS: Casings made from windpipes or throat membranes of animals, in which snuff is packed.

WEAVER'S KNOT: A small flat knot that is used to join ends of yarn.

WEB: Excess metal which has been forced into holes at the parting line of dies during a forging operation.

WEBBING STRETCHER: A handtool used to stretch webbing across furniture seat frames.

WEIGHTING: The treatment of silk with a solution containing tin to make it heavier.

WELT BAR: A bar of a knitting machine containing a row of small steel hooks (welt points) that hold the first loops or stitch of fabric until the welt is knitted.

WELT ROD: A small metal rod used to facilitate turning of welt on full-fashioned stockings and to wind hose on takeup roller.

WHITE WATER: Water separated from paper pulp during processing. It contains varying amounts of reclaimable fibers, fillers, dyestuffs, and other elements.

WHITING COMPOUND: A mixture of powdered chalk and liquid glue used to form wood sealer or priming base for further application of paint.

WICK: Strands of asbestos twisted together and used for making asbestos rope, packing for steam valves, and as a seal for oven or furnace doors.

WINDUP RACK: A rack that has a continuous drive action which winds long lengths of material into a roll after material has passed through a machine.

WIREBOUND BOX: A box made of veneer held together by wire stapled to the box section.

WORD: An ordered set of CHARACTERS which occupies one STORAGE location and is treated by the COMPUTER circuits as a unit and transferred as such. Ordinarily a WORD is treated by the control unit as an INSTRUCTION and by the arithmetic unit as a quantity. WORD lengths may be fixed or variable, depending on the particular COMPUTER.

WORM: A power-driven cutting bead, rotating in such a manner that it moves forward through a pipe, cutting scale, chemical deposits, and other residue from the wall of the pipe.

YARN CARRIER: In flat knitting, the sliding frame above the needlebeds that hold the cams and yarn guides and carries them to and fro.

Z-CALENDER: See FOUR-ROLL CALENDER.

CPSIA information can be obtained
at www.ICGtesting.com
Printed in the USA
LVHW022051171219
640814LV00022B/544